SECOND-TERM BLUES

SECOND-TERM BLUES
HOW GEORGE W. BUSH HAS GOVERNED

JOHN C. FORTIER

AND

NORMAN J. ORNSTEIN

EDITORS

AMERICAN ENTERPRISE INSTITUTE
BROOKINGS INSTITUTION PRESS
Washington, D.C.

Library of Congress Cataloging-in-Publication data
Second-term blues : how George W. Bush has governed /
John C. Fortier and Norman J. Ornstein, editors.
p.   cm.
Summary: "Illuminates the priorities, governing tendencies, and leadership style of a
president in his second term. Reveals how Bush's foreign policy defines and restricts
his presidency, dissects America's changing political mood and considers how the
president's personal style fits into that milieu, and defines his executive style"—
Provided by publisher.
Includes bibliographical references and index.
ISBN-13: 978-0-8157-2884-9 (cloth : alk. paper)
ISBN-10: 0-8157-2884-0 (cloth : alk. paper)
1. United States—Politics and government—2001– 2. Bush, George W.
(George Walker), 1946– I. Fortier, John C. II. Ornstein, Norman J. III. Title.
JK275.S425 2007
973.931092—dc22   2007006938

1 2 3 4 5 6 7 8 9
The paper used in this publication meets minimum requirements of the
American National Standard for Information Sciences—Permanence of Paper
for Printed Library Materials: ANSI Z39.48-1992.

Typeset in Sabon

Composition by Cynthia Stock
Silver Spring, Maryland

Printed by R. R. Donnelley
Harrisonburg, Virginia

Contents

Preface

Before the 2000 election, Norman Ornstein, Thomas Mann, and I began to reflect on an essential element that was missing from the media coverage of presidential election campaigns.

The media spend most of their time covering the daily activities of the candidates—their campaign stops, the debates, the ups and downs of poll numbers. Through shouted press questions, debates, interest group scorecards and questionnaires, the media are also good at ferreting out the political positions of the candidates, even detailed stances on very specific policy areas.

What the media generally miss, however, is perhaps of greatest importance: how the candidates would govern as president, if elected. Essentially the coverage of campaigns is all about campaigning, not about the four years of governing that would follow or the clues in the past performance of candidates that would reveal their governing styles.

The lack of media coverage about governing is especially surprising because our recent presidents have been strangers to

Washington. Only one president in the past thirty years, George H. W. Bush, had ever held an official job in Washington before being sworn in as president.

Voters should know about the positions and political ideologies of presidential candidates. In many ways, the trial-by-fire of a long and grueling campaign tells us about the strength of candidates, their ability to handle ups and downs, whether they can communicate a message, and if they can run an organization. But we should also know much more about how they would deal with a legislature, work with their own and other political parties, manage a White House, set priorities among legislative agenda items, and inspire a country. And the best source of wisdom on the governing qualities of the candidates is past performance in public service. How did Jimmy Carter's status as a maverick governor affect his dealings with the Georgia legislature that was controlled by his own Democratic Party. What did Ronald Reagan's gubernatorial staff look like? How did Bill Clinton rebound from the adversity of a defeat for reelection as governor? All of these are relevant, perhaps essential, questions to ask before entrusting someone for four years with the executive branch of the most powerful country in the world.

In addition to some sense of a candidate's past, a thoughtful observer of the governing qualities of a president should know something about governing as president in general and of the specific conditions that might face the next president. How would Clinton's experience as Arkansas governor with a heavily Democratic legislature transfer to Washington, where Republicans were a significant force and ultimately controlled Congress? How would George W. Bush's good relationship with the conservative Democratic leadership in Texas play out in a polarized Washington? How would Bush or Al Gore deal with surpluses, or how would Bush or John Kerry confront deficits?

Consideration of the governing qualities of the candidate and the governing situation in Washington can reveal the blind spots a candidate might have or experiences that are readily transferable to the presidency. Bush always was a popular governor; he never had suffered through a major decline in public support. But Clinton faced ups and downs and displayed his Phoenix-like ability to rebound from adversity in Arkansas. Reagan had to deal with a two-party legislature with conservative Republicans and liberal Democrats, a scene that would be familiar in Washington, while Carter and Clinton governed in their states with overwhelming Democratic majorities.

To highlight the issue of governing during the campaign season, we were fortunate to have two foundations generously support projects around the 2000 and 2004 elections. In 2000 the Pew Charitable Trusts funded the American Enterprise Institute–Brookings Institution Transition to Governing Project, which sought to smooth the transition to governing in an era of the permanent campaign. In 2004 the John S. and James L. Knight Foundation funded another AEI-Brookings venture to highlight the news media coverage of governing. This volume was produced because of the Knight Foundation grant.

In both elections, we hosted numerous public panels of colleagues who had worked closely with the presidential candidates and the reporters who covered them in Washington or at home and asked them about various governing qualities of the candidates. In 2000 AEI and Brookings hosted panel sessions in Washington to look at Senator John McCain (R-Ariz.) and former Democratic senator Bill Bradley of New Jersey, and many more to discuss Gore and Bush. In 2001 we followed up with panels about how Bush was governing in his first year. In 2004 we convened panels about how Kerry would govern and how Bush would govern in a second term, highlighting the peculiar challenges for second-term presidents. We followed up in 2005 with a look at how Bush was actually handling his second term. In addition we hosted events at each party's political convention and at several presidential debates. The fruit of these projects has been attention paid to governing because of media coverage of these events, the encouragement of reporters on our panels and in the audience, and the events' transcripts that have been used in academic research.

The materials from these conferences are a supplement to this volume and are available at www.electionreformproject.org.

This volume is another significant part of the larger effort to highlight the governing qualities of presidential candidates. Because there was no incumbent in the 2000 race, we had asked only how the various candidates would govern. But a look in 2004 at the reelection campaign of a sitting president raised other questions. We already knew something about Bush as president, both from our sessions in 2000 on his governance and from seeing his presidency in action. Questions about a second term meant that we had to get at larger problems that all second-term presidents face: how his governing style might differ from his first term and what challenges Bush would face after the election.

In our six-year-old quest to make governing an issue in presidential campaigns, we have found much public receptivity to the subject. Governing can be addressed in a realistic and interesting way that makes sense to politicians, voters, and the academic and journalistic communities. This volume includes articles by several prominent political scientists and journalists who have participated on our panels and who have written extensively about governing. We trust that this volume will encourage future work on governing.

JOHN FORTIER
Washington, D.C.

January 2007

SECOND-TERM BLUES

Introduction

John C. Fortier and Norman J. Ornstein

Second terms have not been good to American presidents. They often are characterized by hubris, burnout, a paucity of new or bold ideas and are plagued by scandal, party infighting, lack of legislative success, and loss of seats in the midterm election.

The Twenty-second Amendment ensures that a reelected president becomes a lame duck, contributing to the diminution of the office in the view of other Washington institutions. But even presidents in office before adoption of the Twenty-second Amendment found that their second terms did not measure up to their first.

George W. Bush has not broken the mold or established a new tradition. He has a bad case of the second-term blues; nearly all of the symptoms are present. This is especially ironic, as the newly reelected Bush, joined by many of his acolytes, argued that the precedents set by second-term presidents did not apply to him. At his second inaugural, he was riding high, pockets filled with political capital, ready to use his election victory to accomplish major reforms to Social Security and the tax code, poetic in his account of America's capacious role in the world.

Consider Bush's situation in relation to presidents, beginning with Franklin Delano Roosevelt, who were reelected to a second term (excluding Harry S. Truman and Lyndon Baines Johnson, who were not).

Hubris

Virtually all second-term presidents start with a healthy dose of hubris, believing that their reelection has proven their critics wrong, that their priorities were given a rocket boost, and, especially for modern ones, that they were left with immense freedom because they no longer have to worry about petty concerns such as getting reelected. FDR is a good example. With his large Democratic majorities, and at the start of an era of Democratic dominance, he aimed high. His second inaugural famously chronicled a nation one-third "ill housed, ill clad, and ill nourished." He sought to combat these problems, extend the New Deal, and wipe away the constraints on his program by the Old Guard. Most famously, he wanted to reshape the Supreme Court of nine old men. While eventually he did get to appoint new justices, in his second term, the Democratic Congress wanted nothing to do with his court packing plan and defeated it soundly. He also failed in his attempt to replace members of the independent Federal Trade Commission. Even more boldly, he tried to defeat conservative Democrats in the 1938 primaries in order to reshape his party but was wildly unsuccessful, which only emboldened them.

Burnout

Fatigue is nearly universally felt in a second term. The presidency is a big job; added to those pressures is the marathon campaign for reelection. Not only is the president under stress, so is his staff. Most have gone four years working eighteen-hour days and now must hope for a second wind. Fatigue is a natural phenomenon. Burnout often weighs on the White House in making day-to-day decisions, but it also leads to turnover and shakeups. A second term often begins with a reshuffle, partly spurred by the desire to channel the energy generated by the election victory into accomplishments, but also because there are tired people seeking to move out, move up, or move to a new position. The pace of White House life makes it less stable after four years in office. Nearly every second-term president has replaced his chief of staff in the year or two after the election; Ronald Reagan and Bill Clinton did so at the beginning of their second terms, Bush and Dwight D. Eisenhower before the second midterm elections.

Lack of New Ideas

Second terms also are characterized by a paucity of new ideas. If presidents have big ideas, they usually raise them in the first term. Sometimes they succeed. If they fail to implement their grandiose notions in the first term, it is rare that conditions will change to make it more likely that they will succeed in the second. Since reelections are affirmations of the status quo, voters tend not to err on the side of revolutionary change, contributing to an even more unfavorable climate for big ideas. The one striking exception to this rule is Reagan, whose push for tax reform materialized in his second term and became one of his signature achievements. This occurred in part because he laid the political and substantive foundation late in his first term, made the ideas a true centerpiece of his reelection campaign, and built a plan on broad bipartisan support, drawing on the ideas of Democratic icons Bill Bradley, a senator from New Jersey, and Dick Gephardt, a representative from Missouri, and relying on staunch support from the powerful

Democratic chairman of the House Ways and Means Committee, Dan Rostenkowski of Illinois.

Scandal

Scandal haunts second-term presidents: Sherman Adams's vicuña coat, Watergate, Iran-contra, Monica Lewinsky. It is not simply that scandals occur in second terms because presidents have been around longer, or are more tempted, or simply succumb to the law of averages and find wrongdoing eventually uncovered. First-term scandals are not unknown. But, generally, scandal needs time to germinate, to be uncovered, and to be regarded by the press and public as timely or relevant. Many of the most famous second-term scandals began in the first term and were suppressed successfully by the White House, enabling the presidents to win reelection and avoid embarrassment. But the process of skillful suppression often contains the seed of destruction—the coverup becomes the scandal more than the original offense. Just as important, scandal in the executive branch is highlighted, prolonged, and exploited by congressional investigations. With the exception of FDR, every second-term president since the Civil War has faced a Congress with at least one chamber controlled by the other party. In a second term, let the investigations begin.

Party Infighting

Party unity suffers in second terms. Successful first-term presidents—for example, those who can win reelection—are able to secure the consistent support of their party in Congress, getting factions to muffle their differences, to be team players in order to get things done, and to win reelection. The president's partisans are made to see that their fate, and the fate of the president, is inextricably linked—if he succeeds, so will they; if he fails, so will they. At the same time, a successful president is able to keep his party's ideological base inside the tent by convincing the base to cut him some slack so he can win reelection.

A second-term president faces a very different dynamic. His supporters know that this may be their last chance to get what they want, so there often is impatience with presidents, which is heightened by unrealistic expectations. His partisans in Congress realize that his fate and theirs are now separated—they are up for reelection in the coming midterms, which are historically deeply damaging to the president's party, while he will not be up for election again. The willingness to get distance from the president—and to intensify that distance if he suffers public disapproval—increases geometrically. The ideological base, at the same time, calls in its chits now that the president no longer has an excuse to move away from its priorities or issues.

With these difficulties, it is not surprising that second-term presidents are less legislatively successful than first-termers. Of course, legislation does get passed; Congress has its own agenda to work on, and there have been notable second-term breakthroughs such as the 1986 tax reform act for Reagan mentioned earlier. But, generally, a second-term president is less legislatively successful and, more important, less in charge of the legislative agenda.

Salvation Abroad

Presidents experience a honeymoon at the start of their first term, when there is at least a greater prospect for party unity and often less vociferous opposition. There is also a sense of urgency for a president to get some things accomplished that he can campaign on for reelection. But a second-term president has diminished command of the domestic legislative agenda. And, for the most part, presidents realize their predicament and try to seal their legacy with foreign policy accomplishments. They do this because presidents feel more comfortable on the world stage and know they can act in foreign policy more independently of Congress, the news media, and other Washington forces. Reagan and Clinton were more active and more lauded in foreign policy in their second terms. And foreign policy achievements often proceed on a separate track from the president's troubles at home. In 1987 alone, Reagan dealt with a Senate in Democratic hands, faced Iran-contra investigations by both the Tower Commission and Congress, and fired his chief of staff. But he also famously called on Soviet leader Mikhail S. Gorbachev to "tear down this wall" in Berlin and negotiated a historic arms control agreement with the Soviets. Clinton's heavy involvement in the Northern Ireland and Middle East peace initiatives, military action in the Balkans, Iraq, and Somalia were juxtaposed with battles with the Republican Congress and the Lewinsky scandal.

Midterm Losses

Finally, a second-term president nearly always faces bad news in the midterm election. For more than 150 years, until 1998, no second-term president's party had gained seats in either the House or Senate at the midterm election. Clinton broke this string in 1998 when Democrats picked up five House seats; the Senate numbers did not change. But there were two peculiar circumstances for Clinton. His party had lost so badly in his first midterm election that there was less to lose, and the impeachment and trial of the president rallied what might otherwise have been a divided Democratic Party.

In general, a loss in the second midterm election has several disheartening qualities for a president. It means a smaller majority, or, in many cases, the loss of a majority in Congress. And bad news with only two years left in a second term is dispiriting to the president's party. The rosy prospects for the future that marked the beginning of the first term seem like a distant memory for a lame duck president with only two years to go and faced with a less friendly Congress. Scandals are more likely to be investigated by Congress if the opposing party takes control, and the sense of waiting out a president grows. Finally, as political scientist Charles O. Jones has pointed out, midterm elections are usually (although not always fairly) viewed as a referendum on the president, and if the election does not go the president's way, the dominant story in the news is defeat of the president with only two years to go.

Bush: Hubris

Bush's second term already has exhibited most of these distinctions. While partisans may disagree about the use of the term "hubris," clearly Bush has been a confident president, and his confidence about the prospects for his second term far exceeded the reality. In his first term, Bush maintained the reputation of being a strong leader, which was well deserved for his actions under fire in the aftermath of 9/11. But as Bush's popularity has waned, Congress, the news media, and other institutions have been more vocal in arguing that the Bush White House was too strong a defender of executive powers and did not consult Congress on important matters. The perception of strength of leadership also waned because the president was not decisive in responding to Hurricane Katrina and did not dominate the legislative and policy agenda in Washington as he had in his first term.

Bush: Burnout

The Bush team also has faced the burnout issue. Speculation arose that administration lapses over the federal response to Katrina were exacerbated by an exhausted White House, especially including Chief of Staff Andrew H. Card Jr., who had a longer tenure than nearly all of his predecessors, and Karl Rove, who had full-time portfolios as chief political adviser and deputy chief of staff for domestic policy. A little over a year into his second term, Bush embarked on the first real White House shakeup. Before that, major figures had left the White House—Karen Hughes for Texas, and Condoleezza Rice, Alberto Gonzales, and Margaret Spellings to head executive departments—but no major figure had joined the circle of close Bush advisers. The replacement of Card with Joshua B. Bolten seemed at first a mere reshuffling of chairs. But the subsequent changes involving a new communications director, a new Office of Management and Budget director to replace Bolten, a new Treasury secretary, the reassignment of Rove to focus exclusively on political matters, in particular the 2006 midterm elections, and several other changes made this a real shakeup.

Bush had intended his second term to be marked by two big domestic agenda ideas, but not new ideas: Social Security reform and tax reform. Bush had made these issues part of his campaign agenda in 2000, but, once elected, it became clear that these were tough issues to tackle, particularly Social Security. So they were put off until after the reelection. Bush surprised Washington pundits by being able to campaign successfully on allocating a portion of Social Security payroll taxes to private accounts. Social Security was once called the "third rail" of politics: touch it and you were dead.

But while he was twice able to campaign on the issue, Social Security reform was not ready for congressional action. Unlike the start of his first term as Texas governor or his presidential start in 2001, when new key issues moved from the campaign immediately into the legislative process, Social Security reform had been studied and talked about until 2005. But it still did not have enough of a constituency on Capitol Hill, even among Republicans. So the issue sat while Bush tried to go directly to the country with his message. But it never gained the legislative traction that moved the issues he emphasized in his first term.

Bush: Scandal

In Bush's second term, scandal was also in the air in Washington. As Republicans controlled the presidency and Congress, it is not surprising that the lion's share of scandals was in their camp. Most notable were congressional scandals, and the one involving lobbyist Jack Abramoff was the most significant. Abramoff connections led to the resignation of House Majority Leader Tom DeLay and the conviction of GOP congressman Bob Ney of Ohio.

In addition, there was the case of Republican congressman Duke Cunningham of California, who pleaded guilty to conspiracy to commit bribery, among other charges. His acceptance of favors and maintaining a cozy relationship with lobbyists who dealt with military construction led the FBI to investigate other members of Congress. Finally, the scandal involving congressman Mark Foley of Florida, while more of a congressional matter, hit Bush's Republican colleagues in the House hard because it added to other doubts voters had about Republicans and surfaced only about a month before election day.

The Abramoff scandal also touched on the Bush administration, especially in the case of the executive director of the General Services Administraton, David Safavian, who was convicted of having received favors from Abramoff, his former boss, and having provided insider information on contracts that might have been helpful to the former lobbyist.

But the scandal that hit the White House hardest was the Joseph Wilson/Valerie Plame affair pursued by Special Prosecutor Patrick

Fitzgerald, which raised questions beyond the allegations of improper release of classified information. Critics have asked whether this is an example of an administration trying to silence its critics on the war in Iraq. I. Lewis "Scooter" Libby Jr., the former chief of staff to Vice President Dick Cheney, was indicted. The scandal also threatened to implicate Rove, the president's closest political adviser, although he was not ultimately targeted by the prosecutor.

Bush: Unity

Republican Party unity in the Bush administration has swung wildly from the Dr. Jekyll–like reflexive loyalty of the first term to the Mr. Hyde–like declared congressional independence from the White House in the second term. Few who studied the Bush administration would have predicted that congressional Republicans with such a small majority would be able to hold together as regularly as they did in Bush's first four years. The unity was extraordinary. For Republicans to win on a party line vote in the House of Representatives in 2001, they could only afford five defectors from their ranks. The Senate began with a 50-50 tie, broken by the vice president, but soon turned to a one-seat Democratic majority when Senator Jim Jeffords (I-Vt.) left the Republican Party. In all of the forty years that Democrats controlled the House, they never had a working majority as slim as the 2001–02 Republican Congress.

And Bush more or less relied on his Republican majority. After the initial No Child Left Behind Act, which was passed with significant support from key Democratic leaders, most of Bush's agenda was accomplished along partisan lines, sometimes attracting some Democratic votes but often relying on arm-twisting of key Republican House members to achieve one-vote majorities on important issues. The reasons for the unity on the Republican side were many. It was the first time Republicans had controlled the presidency and both chambers of Congress since the 1950s. September 11 added to the sense of national purpose. House leaders were extremely skilled in counting votes and pulling out close votes, sometimes with tough tactics such as holding open votes for long periods or cutting generous deals to sway wavering Republicans. Also, significantly, the two political parties have become extremely polarized over the past thirty years. Where once there were many conservative southern Democrats and liberal northeastern Republicans, today there is nearly perfect separation between the parties, with few moderating voices. This was different from the situation Governor Bush faced in Texas, where he had to govern with a legislature partly controlled by conservative Democrats and where he often worked across party lines.

The unity of the first term makes the dissent of the second even more striking. Democratic opposition was stiffer to Bush as political allegiances hardened, and Democrats began to make many of the arguments that Republicans had made in the final days of their minority status. Still, despite their unity, Democrats had little input, especially in the House, where Republicans governed with their own narrow majority.

Opposition

But more significant than an invigorated opposition was the willingness of a Republican Congress to oppose a president of its own party. The criticisms began in earnest in the summer of 2005, when conservative budget hawks, concerned with the rise in domestic spending, flexed their strength and let the leadership know that their votes would come at the cost of restraining spending. This independent Republican populism surfaced again in the case of

Supreme Court nominee Harriet Miers, immigration reform, and the Dubai ports deal. Moderate Republicans found they could oppose their leadership on issues such as drilling in the Arctic National Wildlife Refuge. The administration also angered House Speaker J. Dennis Hastert of Illinois with the treatment of Porter Goss, a former member of Congress from Florida who was dismissed as CIA chief, and the FBI's raid on the congressional offices of Representative William J. Jefferson (D-La.).

Bush: Midterm Losses

With the midterm elections came expected losses. The loss of thirty seats in the House was not as large as the more than fifty that Republicans and Newt Gingrich gained in 1994. But examining these elections more carefully, 2006 looked a lot like 1994. All of the major political indicators (for example, the president's job approval rating, the generic ballot test, and polls showing whether the public thought the country was on the right or wrong track) significantly favored Democrats all year long. And the smaller number of House seats lost can be explained: the Republicans defended fewer open seats, ran fewer freshmen, and had fewer Republicans sitting in Democratic districts than did Democrats in 1994.

The election was an across-the-board loss for Bush and the Republicans. No incumbent Democrat lost in the House or Senate. In fact, in the House, only six incumbent Democrats won less than 55 percent of the vote. Democrats netted six governorships and large numbers of state legislators and state houses.

Bush's Blues

Bush's second-term blues are evident and to some extent could be predicted based on the history of past second-term presidents. But it is striking how Bush defined himself and set out a governing strategy that was to overcome inherent second-term problems. In his own words, Bush reiterated his theory of "political capital" and how he could spend it to overcome these larger second-term forces.

As far back as his time in Texas, Bush defined his governing style in terms of "political capital." For Bush, this meant that a leader could not sit on his popularity or bask in his triumphs but had to put that capital to work on other policy endeavors or else that capital would waste away.

The negative example that illustrates the use of political capital is the presidency of George H. W. Bush, who reached the stratosphere of public approval after the U.S. victory in the 1991 Gulf War. From a 90 percent favorable rating in the polls, Bush dropped like a stone and eventually lost the presidency to Clinton. Bush's Republican critics called him the "in-box" president because he dealt with issues that were put on his agenda but did not have a forceful political agenda of his own. For George W. Bush, the sin of the father was that he did not use his popularity after the Gulf War for political and policy purposes.

George W. Bush has followed the motto that "winners win." When he was given accolades for his initial policy successes as governor, when he finally was elected to his first term as president (even in a controversial election), in the aftermath of 9/11, after his victory in the 2002 midterm elections, and after the initial successes of the Iraq War, Bush used these victories to press for more of his agenda. Whether it was a new school financing plan in Texas, tax cuts, or a Department of Homeland Security, Bush did not sit on his laurels.

It was this theory of political capital that informed his plans for a second term. Two days after his reelection, Bush said:

Let me put it to you this way: I earned capital in the campaign, political capital, and now I intend to spend it. It is my style. That's what happened in the—after the 2000 election, I earned some capital. I've earned capital in this election—and I'm going to spend it for what I told the people I'd spend it on, which is—you've heard the agenda: Social Security and tax reform, moving this economy forward, education, fighting and winning the war on terror.

Bush's understanding of his own political capital was astute. But it also relied on his always having been a somewhat popular governor or president. Before his 2004 reelection, Bush did not suffer the wild ups and downs that Clinton did throughout his governorship and presidency. When Bush's popularity began to drop significantly in 2005, the theory of political capital, his grip on narrow Republican majorities, and the public's perception of his strong leadership began to suffer.

Perhaps under different circumstances, Bush might have been able to keep his string of victories going, expending political capital to get more from his accomplishments. But the end of that string means that Bush must confront a phenomenon more common to second-term presidents—dealing with Congress, the public, and other institutions from a position of weakness, struggling to regain past popularity.

This book looks at how Bush governs, especially through the lens of his governing style in a second term. There are, of course, stylistic continuities, but the challenge to understanding how a president governs is a combination of his own governing qualities meshed with the circumstances before him. How Bush governs in a second term is about Bush and his environment.

The authors in this book are political scientists and journalists, but not ordinary ones in the least. Political scientists Fred Greenstein and Charles O. Jones are thoughtful historical and institutional thinkers, but they are also intimately familiar with the day-to-day governing of Bush and other presidents. Our journalists, Dan Balz, Carla Anne Robbins, and David Sanger are not only filing stories to make deadlines, but they have a long record of thinking more broadly and comparatively over different presidencies. They have the knowledge and personal access to presidents and their staffs and a longer-term understanding about governing. All of the essays in this collection trace Bush's governing in a second term through domestic and foreign policy issues, in relation to his first term and to other presidents, and show a deep understanding of how presidents operate with the many other actors and institutions in Washington that matter.

Bush's Ambitious Second-Term Agenda Hits Reality

2

Dan Balz

President Bush began his second term with grand ambitions and great expectations. Abroad he set his sights on continuing a transformation of American foreign policy and, by design, the world, through his campaign against terrorism and his vision of spreading democracy to Iraq and the greater Middle East. He established the tone in his inaugural address, setting out a generations-long goal of ending tyranny in the world. At home he hoped to continue his makeover of the political landscape and to further his goal of cementing in place durable Republican majorities in Congress and the state houses. He placed the restructuring of Social Security at the top of his domestic agenda, seeking to create a permanent legacy by radically restructuring the government's retirement insurance program through the introduction of private savings accounts.

Two years later Bush was a dramatically diminished figure. Republicans suffered a significant rebuke when Democrats captured control of the House and Senate in the midterm elections of

2006 that became a referendum on the Bush presidency, the Iraq war and the performance of the 109th Congress. The president came under pressure from Democrats and Republicans alike to redesign his Iraq policy. Neoconservatives who had enthusiastically argued for the invasion of Iraq recanted their support for the administration. Social Security reform, Bush's signature second-term initiative, long ago had been declared dead. The Republican coalition fractured on immigration, spending, and social issues. The early stirrings of the 2008 presidential election guaranteed that Bush would face competition even within his own party for attention and setting the agenda.

When historians look back for reasons to explain the precipitous decline, they are likely to focus on the year 2005 and how mistakes, misjudgments, bad luck, and a war gone awry drained power and public support from Bush's presidency. What happened in the 2006 midterm elections seemed utterly predictable by the end of 2005. The first year of Bush's second term will be remembered as his *annus horribilis,* a year that marked the collapse of the balancing act Bush had managed with relative success during his first four years in office.

Through his first term Bush was both the most divisive president of the modern era and a politician who managed nonetheless to enlarge the Republican Party's governing majorities, largely through a series of skillful election campaigns. He deftly managed this seeming contradiction, although he was aided considerably by how the terrorist attacks of September 11, 2001, reshaped the country. But what worked in Bush's first term failed to work in his second. Traits once seen as strengths became weaknesses. The "conviction politician" of the 2004 campaign who attracted support by saying voters knew where he stood even if they didn't always agree with him increasingly came to be seen as inflexible and unwilling to adjust his war policy until the damage had been done. The politician who routinely catered most to his conservative base—and there was no greater symbol of that in 2005 than his decision to fly back to Washington to sign legislation that overrode the jurisdiction of Florida courts in the anguished case of Terri Schiavo—finally lost support among moderates and independent voters. The president who showed Republicans how to win elections by energizing the GOP faithful ran into problems pursuing a partisan legislative strategy, which sought to enact a boldly conservative agenda with the slimmest of partisan majorities. The leader who prided himself on big-picture governance and delegation of power learned the cost of that approach when he could not force action on Social Security in a recalcitrant House. The White House team that prided itself on discipline, planning, and execution proved lacking in flexibility and did not readjust quickly enough when Hurricane Katrina hit the Gulf Coast. White House officials sent the president west for prearranged events just as New Orleans was filling up with water. Katrina not only battered the Gulf Coast, it devastated support for Bush's presidency.

The changing fortunes in Bush's first year after his reelection were captured at two press conferences roughly eleven months apart. The first came in November 2004, two days after Bush had won 51 percent of the vote in defeating Senator John F. Kerry (D-Mass.). The president was in an ebullient mood—upbeat, focused, even playful as he bantered with the White House press corps. It seemed clear that winning a second term—doing what his father had failed to do—had filled him with newfound buoyancy and self-assurance. Presidential historian Fred Greenstein said he saw a difference between the reelected Bush and the inexperienced governor who had arrived in Washington four years earlier. "I think he has come to fill that space," he said.

Karl Rove, the architect of the reelection victory, said of his boss not long after the reelection, "He's grown to have a comfort with exercising the levers available to him. He understands the office better. He's comfortable with it. Second, he now has a series of relationships, internationally with [foreign leaders]. He knows them, understands them, he has taken the measure of them in a way you can only do if you're up close. Third, he is more acutely aware that while a president can set an agenda—and it's vital you do so—that history has a way of intruding on you. Things happen."

At the postelection press conference, Bush projected a sense of urgency about his second term. "I earned capital in the campaign, political capital, and now I intend to spend it," he told reporters. "It is my style."

The second press conference was in October 2005. As Rove had foreshadowed, history had intruded on Bush's presidency. Many things happened, driving Bush's approval ratings below 40 percent, disrupting his agenda, and causing his Republican coalition to fragment. The Rose Garden press conference was a far more difficult encounter than the postelection session. Reporters peppered the president with challenging questions. Bush appeared defensive rather than upbeat. The commentary afterward noted that his customary swagger was missing. Toward the end of the session, Ed Chen, then of the *Los Angeles Times,* reminded Bush what he had said the previous November. "How much political capital do you have left?" he asked. To which Bush replied, with perhaps forced emphasis, "Plenty." This time his answer was greeted with skepticism.

Bush's advisers often describe Bush as a consequential figure—controversial to be sure and admittedly anathema to a portion of the population, but a leader whose ambitions and achievements eventually will be recognized by historians as significant. His critics have a far less charitable view of Bush. They see him as a leader who squandered the unity of 9/11, who led America into war in Iraq under false pretenses, who badly mismanaged the invasion's aftermath, and who damaged the country's reputation in the eyes of much of the world. Final judgments of Bush's presidency will come after he leaves office, but at this point, the damage to his legacy from Iraq obviously has been substantial. History suggests that he will have difficulty turning around impressions that he squandered U.S. power and prestige, although history is not always a reliable guide.

The presidency is inherently a resilient office. External events, unpredictable as they are, can quickly reorder a nation's priorities—and a president's standing—as they did on the morning of September 11. Other presidents have rebounded after severe problems in their second terms. One need go back no farther than Ronald Reagan's second term, when the Iran-contra scandal drove the president's approval ratings sharply downward and threatened permanent damage to his presidency. By admitting his mistakes, accepting responsibility, and cleaning out his White House staff, Reagan successfully restarted his presidency. Still, Bush faces two difficult years. He reorganized his White House staff in 2006 and still was not able to head off midterm losses. After the elections, he accepted the resignation of Secretary of Defense Donald Rumsfeld, which many in both parties had called for months—even years— earlier. But the damage was already done to his presidency.

The very skills that have made Bush such a successful, even feared, political candidate came with a longer-term cost. On the campaign trail, he projected a kind of unwavering assurance that many voters found more appealing than the personalities of either Al Gore or Kerry. That same style worked less effectively in the arena of governing, where presidential lubricant is needed as much as steadfast conviction. Bush's mediocre relations with Congress were a marked contrast to the rapport he established with members of the Texas legislature when he was governor.

Bush championed policies designed for their political appeal not to the nation at large but to smaller segments of the electorate—

conservative Roman Catholics, Latino small business owners, younger workers worried about retirement. The goal was to add a percentage point or two to his electoral support. What worked in campaigns, however, did not result in a mandate for legislative action, and Social Security remains Exhibit A. He has pursued a political strategy aimed at capitalizing on the polarization in American politics and has been the key instrument in helping the Republicans gain seats in both the 2002 and 2004 elections. But that approach—both stylistically and substantively—left him early in his second term with narrowing public support for some of his major policies and declining confidence in his leadership, not only among Democrats but increasingly among independents. In a *Washington Post*–ABC News poll taken in October 2005, Bush's approval rating among independent voters stood at just 33 percent.

This is a president who has emphasized the power of strong leadership but often has fallen short in the art of persuasion and education. He has spoken often about bipartisanship while following a governing strategy dependent on united Republican support, to the exclusion of the Democrats. It is a strategy that left his opponents deeply alienated and more rigid in their opposition. With Democrats now in charge of Congress, his—and their—commitment to bipartisanship will be tested again.

Perhaps understandably as the Iraq war went from bad to worse and the country grew dissatisfied with his leadership, Bush projected a grimmer personality. Under pressure his buoyancy and wisecracking sometimes gave way to irritation and impatience, particularly with those who challenged or questioned his leadership. In the middle of his reelection campaign, Bush ran into an old political ally who wondered aloud how the president was coping with perceptions that he had become a divider, not a uniter. Bush responded tartly that he was busy trying to change the world in the face of terrorist threats. If people seemed not to understand, or were impatient or unhappy about that, so be it.

Second-Term Blues

History reminds us that presidential second terms rarely are as successful as first terms. At times in 2005, Bush's presidency appeared to have become a case study of that maxim. His administration suffered at different points along the way from ineffectiveness, incompetence, political overreaching, public disaffection, insularity, signs of staff weariness, and cracks in the GOP's governing coalition.

Newly reelected administrations often suffer from the hubris that comes from defeating determined opponents in consecutive elections. For Bush's team the exhilaration of winning reelection under extraordinarily difficult circumstances must have been particularly seductive. Bush ran against a headwind of declining support for a war whose principal justification—the threat of weapons of mass destruction—had proven to be false, and an economy that had failed to produce any net new jobs during his first four years in office. After winning a majority of the popular vote in 2004, Bush and his team had every right to see themselves as political masters of the universe—and every reason to resist acting on that feeling by their own reading of history. But they did not always act on that evidence.

Second terms often prove more challenging for a host of reasons. One is that a reelected president starts not with a clean slate but with an agenda of leftovers and unsolved problems, hard cases unresolved during the first four years, or second-tier initiatives that lack the glamour or broad political appeal of those pushed at the start of a presidency. Bush began his second term plagued by an Iraq policy that had gone off track almost immediately after U.S. forces deposed Saddam Hussein and liberated Baghdad. There would be no easy fix. Domestically, Social Security rose to the top of his agenda in large part because it was too risky and too difficult to deal with in his first term.

Second terms often are plagued by scandal. Richard Nixon was forced to resign in his second term because of Watergate, and both Ronald Reagan (Iran-contra) and Bill Clinton (Monica Lewinsky and impeachment) found their second terms similarly clouded by such humiliations. Special Prosecutor Patrick Fitzgerald's investigation into how CIA agent Valerie Plame was publicly unmasked did not touch Bush directly but proved to be a significant distraction to his White House. Fitzgerald indicted Vice President Dick Cheney's chief of staff, I. Lewis "Scooter" Libby, in October 2005, forcing Libby's resignation. But fears inside the White House that Rove might be indicted disappeared in 2006 when the special prosecutor cleared him. Later it was revealed that Richard Armitage, the former deputy secretary of state, provided the original leak to columnist Robert Novak, which badly dented the theory that there was a White House plot to expose Plame's identity. This came long after the harm was done in terms of lost momentum.

Scandals involving Republicans, however, proved terribly damaging politically in the midterm elections. House Majority Leader Tom DeLay of Texas was indicted for alleged misconduct in the redistricting battle that gave the GOP five additional seats in the House in 2004. Republican House member Randy "Duke" Cunningham of California pleaded guilty to taking bribes and resigned from Congress. Republican House member Bob Ney of Ohio pleaded guilty in the corruption investigation involving Jack Abramoff, the powerful and well-connected GOP lobbyist. In October 2006, Mark Foley of Florida resigned from the House in disgrace after sexually graphic e-mails and instant messages with a former House page surfaced. Those cases tainted the GOP majority in Washington and cost the Republicans seats in the midterms.

Fatigue often saps the imagination and energy of second-term administrations, which is another reason they are rarely as productive as first terms. Few presidential staffs lived under as much tension in their first four years as Bush's, from the national trauma of 9/11, to the controversial decision to take the country to war in Iraq in March 2003, to the intensity of a lengthy and brutal reelection campaign. Bush and his inner circle operated with the constant threat of new terrorist attacks in the United States, under the cloud of a steady stream of combat deaths in Iraq, and in a political environment that radicalized Bush opponents into Bush haters.

After the 2004 election, Rove's Office of Strategic Initiatives undertook a study of previous second terms to help prepare the president and his staff for the challenges and problems that typically afflict reelected presidents. White House advisers argued that, despite past history, there was every reason to believe the second term would be more successful and productive than the first.

On the eve of Bush's second inauguration, a senior White House official described the cabinet changes as evidence of Bush's determination to make a fresh start. Bush shuffled part of his cabinet, sending White House counsel Alberto Gonzales to the Justice Department, sending domestic adviser Margaret Spellings to the Education Department, and, in the biggest move of all, accepting the resignation of Secretary of State Colin Powell and replacing him with National Security Adviser Condoleezza Rice. "He wants to demonstrate the same vigor, passion and commitment [as at the beginning of his first term]," a senior White House official said at the time. Bush's personnel changes, he added, were meant to send the message that "I don't take my second term for granted."

Outsiders saw a different pattern in the personnel shifts. They argued that by moving trusted White House advisers to the cabinet, Bush was looking less for a fresh start and more to assert a tighter grip on the agencies. They concluded that he wanted no repeats of the embarrassments generated by his first Treasury secretary, Paul O'Neill. Nor was he looking for a continuation of the warfare among Powell's State Department and the Pentagon and

Cheney's office. At Education and Justice, Spellings and Gonzales were far more trusted by the White House than their predecessors had been. There were other cabinet and White House staff changes: a new Commerce Department secretary, a new Health and Human Services secretary, new White House national security, economic, and domestic policy advisers. But the clearest sign that Bush was not ready to signal a serious attempt to shake up his administration and start his second term on a fresh note was the decision to retain Rumsfeld. That was evidence that, at the beginning of his second term, Bush had interpreted his reelection victory as a mandate to continue the path he had followed in his first four years.

The Unraveling

The opening days of Bush's second term brought success in Iraq and the anticipation of more, but a confluence of events may have led to a critical strategic miscalculation by the president's White House team. Bush's decision to turn away from Iraq and refocus his attention to pushing Congress to enact a radical overhaul of Social Security cost his administration on two fronts. The more he talked about Social Security, the less Americans were buying and the less Congress seemed willing to embrace his proposals. The less he talked about Iraq, the more Americans—overwhelmed by daily reports of U.S. casualties, insurgent attacks, and suicide bombings—turned sour on the conflict.

For Bush, the reelection campaign had settled the question of whose vision for Iraq the American people preferred. "We had an accountability moment, and that's called the 2004 elections," Bush told *Washington Post* reporters Michael Fletcher and Jim Vande-Hei in a pre-inauguration interview. "The American people listened to different assessments made about what was taking place in Iraq, and they looked at the two candidates, and chose me." The truth was more complicated, but Bush's conclusion may have persuaded him that he could spend less time than he had in 2004 making the case for his Iraq policy, which in turn may have comforted him that he could safely shift his attention in early 2005 to Social Security, the centerpiece of a domestic agenda that had been overshadowed during much of his first term by terrorism and war.

But a parallel reality was beginning to take shape in the weeks after Bush's victory. Far from receiving a significant boost in public opinion, the president enjoyed one of the shortest honeymoons on record. Within weeks of his successful campaign, his approval rating had slipped just below 50 percent, leaving him lower than any reelected president in the post–World War II era. "The question is what happened to the honeymoon?" Frank Newport, editor of the Gallup survey, told the *Los Angeles Times*. If the president's advisers hoped for even a short-term boost to help launch the second term, polls showing Bush 10 to 20 points lower in his approval ratings than Dwight D. Eisenhower, Nixon, Reagan, and Clinton demonstrated that the elections had done little to lessen the partisan divisions that had plagued Bush throughout much of his presidency.

At the same time, Democrats—weakened in so many ways by their election defeats—nonetheless were coalescing to challenge the newly reelected president. They were determined to put up a united front against his major initiatives, particularly Social Security. The Democrats' posture represented a departure from that of four years earlier when, after the disputed Florida recount and the Supreme Court's 5 to 4 decision effectively awarded the presidency to Bush, the Democrats briefly stepped back from the barricades to help enact the two biggest items on the administration's domestic agenda. Senator Edward M. Kennedy (D-Mass.) cooperated with the White House on the No Child Left Behind education bill.

Twelve Democrats, including nine from red states won by Bush in 2000, backed the president's $1.35 trillion tax cut.

By early 2005 Democrats were ready for a fight. They saw Bush's sagging approval ratings as a sign that he was not a force to be feared and they saw no political risk in opposing him. In fact, despite Bush's reelection victory, Democrats could feel the intense hostility toward him on the left. They knew that the party's new powerbase, the net roots activists (symbolized by MoveOn.org, liberal bloggers like Daily Kos, and others in a grassroots progressive community stitched together by e-mail and the Internet) who had sprung up during the 2004 presidential campaign of Howard Dean, demanded confrontation with the president. If there was any political risk, Democratic leaders concluded, it was in cooperating with Bush.

After his reelection Bush had renewed the call he had issued four years earlier for cooperation with the Democrats. This time, however, that extended hand came with an implicit warning that seemed to underscore his belief that, by winning a second term, he expected the opposition to meet him more than half way. "I'll reach out to anyone who shares our goals," he said. Those words angered the Democrats. Iowa senator Tom Harkin signaled the Democrats' attitude as the New Year began. "Usually when you win you try to be magnanimous. But everything we've heard from the president is, 'I've got a mandate,' 'I've got all this political capital,' and, 'We'll work with you as long as you agree with us.' Well, wait a minute, you mean we have to agree to everything before they'll work with us. That's a non-starter." Connecticut senator Christopher J. Dodd said, "There's a much reduced expectation that you can work with this White House or work with this Republican leadership."

Even some red state Democrats, having watched the White House target southerners in 2002 who had supported his big tax cuts—

among them Georgia senator Max Cleland (who was defeated) and Louisiana senator Mary Landrieu (who survived)—had concluded that cooperation with the White House provided no inoculation from Republican attempts to defeat them. Senator Ben Nelson (D-Neb.), who supported all three of Bush's tax cuts, advised the White House to be more flexible. "If he is able to reach out to Democrats in the development of policy rather than having his staff present it as a take-it-or-leave-it basis, it would foster more support," Nelson said. "Last term it seemed like a lot of the time his policy people would work with me and his political people would work on me."

A minor episode at the end of 2004 captured the growing animosity and widening gulf in perceptions between the parties. On December 23 the White House issued a press release announcing that Bush would resubmit to the Senate twenty judicial nominees who had been blocked by Democrats during his first term, including twelve controversial nominees for the federal appeals courts. White House officials said they deliberately had chosen the use of a press release rather than a presidential announcement to make the submissions appear less antagonistic. They also said that Bush had chosen not to send back two of the most controversial nominees from his first term. Their hope was that Democrats would see the gestures as a positive sign of Bush's desire for a different relationship in his second term. Instead, Democrats interpreted the actions as evidence of Bush's determination to use his reelection victory and his larger GOP majority in the Senate to slam through his nominees. Even Senate Judiciary Committee Chairman Arlen Specter (R-Pa.) said he had hoped for a longer interlude to improve relations with the Democrats before being plunged back into the judicial battle. Instead of a lessening of tensions, the two sides began the year farther apart than ever.

These forces were just beginning to swirl around Bush as he prepared for his second inaugural address in late January. He and his advisers believed that opportunities for achieving something of lasting significance were far greater for two-term presidents, and Bush approached his inaugural address with that in mind. He offered an expansive and, to some, a startling vision of his foreign policy, declaring, "It is the policy of the United States to seek and support the growth of democratic movements and institutions in every nation and culture, with the ultimate goal of ending tyranny in our world." He argued that America's security now rested on expanding liberty and freedom around the world and vowed to make the promotion of democracy the centerpiece of his foreign policy objectives. To many who listened it sounded like another dramatic turn in American policy by a president who had introduced the doctrine of preemption in his first term. "We will persistently clarify the choice before every ruler and every nation: the moral choice between oppression, which is always wrong, and freedom, which is eternally right," Bush said in his speech. At another point, he said, "We will encourage reform in other governments by making clear that success in our relations will require the decent treatment of their own people."

The speech represented the most fulsome and idealistic articulation of Bush's foreign policy, which had moved 180 degrees from what Candidate Bush had advocated in 2000, when in a debate with rival Al Gore he rejected nation building and called for greater humility in the way the United States projected its power as the world's lone superpower. Within twenty-four hours of the inaugural address, however, White House officials were rolling back the interpretation that the United States would become more confrontational in its relationships with such countries as Russia, China, Egypt, and Pakistan. They said Bush's speech was an attempt to crystallize, not change, existing policy. "It is not a discontinuity, not a right turn," an administration official told reporters.

Good news followed the inauguration. On January 30, 2005, millions of Iraqis turned out to vote in that country's first free elections in more than half a century, waving purple ink–stained fingers in a show of pride and defiance. It was Baghdad's most festive day since the downfall of Saddam Hussein in April 2003, and the Iraqi citizens' display of courage in the face of suicide bombers and threats to the emerging new government captured the world's imagination. Three days later, Bush delivered his State of the Union address in the afterglow of those elections. The night's most emotional moment came toward the end with a spontaneous and highly symbolic embrace in the balcony of the House chamber between Janet Norwood, whose son Byron had been killed in Iraq, and Safia Taleb al-Suhail, an Iraqi human rights activist whose father had been assassinated by Saddam's intelligence service eleven years earlier. The Iraqi election, coupled with Lebanon's Cedar Revolution and signs of democracy spreading elsewhere in the Middle East, boosted confidence inside the White House that the administration's beleaguered strategy might be working, thereby freeing the president to refocus his energies on his domestic agenda.

On the morning after his State of the Union address, Bush left Washington to begin his campaign to change Social Security. The decision to push Social Security to the forefront of Bush's second-term agenda represented an enormous gamble that some students of Congress felt was ill fated from the start. Louisiana's John Breaux, newly retired from the Senate and recently appointed the co-chairman of a task force asked to recommend ways to overhaul the tax code, said as the campaign began that the president had picked the wrong issue upon which to launch his second term. Breaux believed it could take years to develop a political consensus behind the kind of reforms Bush was advocating. "Social Security is a longer term challenge," he said. "Tax reform is on a faster track." In hindsight, Bush may have made the same kind of mistake Clinton made at the beginning of his administration when he decided to make health care his major priority, rather than welfare reform.

Administration officials were far more sanguine than Breaux about the chances of winning the Social Security battle, at least in their public pronouncements. No matter which official was speaking, the talking points were the same. First, that the public was far ahead of Washington in its recognition of the problem and receptivity to the kind of personal or private accounts Bush wanted. Second, that Republicans who had run for election by advocating partial privatization of the system had won. White House officials had a checklist of such candidates: North Carolina senators Elizabeth Dole and Richard Burr, for example, and, of course, the president himself. "There is not a single Republican member of Congress whose difficulties can be laid at the feet of Social Security," one of Bush's top advisers said early in 2005. Still he did not underestimate the challenge ahead. "Old habits die hard," he said of congressional Republicans.

Almost instantly Bush ran into turbulence. His first trip promoting Social Security restructuring took him to North Dakota, Montana, Nebraska, Arkansas, and Florida—all states with at least one Democratic senator. Instead of following Ben Nelson's advice to work with red state Democrats, however, Bush worked to rally their constituents to put pressure on them to support the president's plan. The *Wall Street Journal*'s Jackie Calmes, in a lengthy analysis written after the prospects for action on Social Security had faded in the fall of 2005, said Bush's campaign-style approach, rather than quiet persuasion, "only stoked the enmity left by his 2002 and 2004 campaigning against moderate Democrats who had backed much of his first-term agenda." Nelson and Bush shared a limousine ride in Omaha, but there were no serious discussions between the two—then or later, Nelson told the *Journal*.

Wherever Bush traveled, protesters organized by a progressive coalition shadowed him with a message of resistance. Back in Washington, a stalemate quickly developed. Senate Minority Leader Harry Reid of Nevada claimed he had enough Democratic votes pledged against private accounts to prevent Republicans from breaking a filibuster. In the House, Republicans were loathe to vote on a plan that could subject them to negative ads in 2006 when there was no prospect it would ever pass the Senate. In a prescient column written just three weeks after Bush's State of the Union address, the *Washington Post*'s David S. Broder made this prediction: "For now, the situation is eerily reminiscent of what faced Bill and Hillary Clinton on their health care reform project in 1994. House Democrats were uncertain the Senate would act and vice versa, so in the end, neither chamber ever held a floor vote on the measure. That is what George Bush could face this time around."

That was February, and for months little changed. Bush and his cabinet charged around the country stumping in behalf of the program, but the public did not warm to his proposal. The president's approval rating on Social Security dropped from 38 percent in January to 34 percent in June, and the lower he went the less incentive Democrats or Republicans had to get serious. At one point Bush offered to raise the cap on that portion of earnings subject to Social Security taxes. Later, hoping to lure Democrats into serious talks, he spoke warmly about a proposal authored by Democrat Robert Pozen—a former head of Fidelity Investments—that included a progressive indexing structure that would have given greater protection to workers at the bottom of the income scale at the expense of wealthier workers. Bush's embrace of Pozen's plan came after an internal debate among his advisers about the wisdom of such a step; his advisers thus were startled when no

Democrat stepped forward to suggest that might be a good trade-off for a modest version of Bush's personal accounts.

Bush's approval rating on Social Security bounced up to 40 percent at the end of August, his best of the year but still too low to spur congressional Republicans to take a risk. Despite all evidence to the contrary, the administration maintained public optimism about congressional action until it was clear that, after Hurricane Katrina had reshuffled the fall legislative agenda, there was no chance of Social Security coming to a vote. At an October 4 press conference, Bush put the matter to rest for the remainder of the year when he said, "When the appetite to address it is—that's going to be up to the members of Congress. I just want to remind people, it's not going away. It's not one of these issues, well, if we don't deal with it now, maybe it will fix itself. It gets worse over time, not better. And I did make some progress convincing the American people there was a problem. And I'm going to continue talking about the problem because I strongly believe that the role of those of us in Washington, one role is to confront problems."

As Bush barnstormed the country in behalf of his Social Security package, the situation in Iraq deteriorated, as did public confidence in the administration's policies. The White House hit one low point in public support for the war in May 2005, and by the next month Bush and his advisers recognized their mistake in failing to make a consistent case for his policy and for his belief that there was hope for success, despite the suicide bombings and U.S. casualties.

Bush aides worried that the public had lost focus on the threat of terrorism. "The farther you get from 9/11, the more difficult it is," one adviser said shortly before Bush went to Fort Bragg, North Carolina, for a June 28 speech defending his policies. Said another adviser, "We need to engage in a consistent effort to make sure Americans recognize the stakes involved in Iraq. All they see are images of chaos and violence." This official argued that it was essential for the president to explain repeatedly the stakes involved in Iraq. "That's a case we have to make because people aren't going to hear it from a lot of other places," he said.

More than five months later Bush was trying again to make that case, after another decline in support for the war and rising opposition from congressional Democrats. But by then the terms of the debate were beginning to shift. Bush was fighting growing public frustration with the lack of progress in Iraq and calls for an exit strategy from his Democratic critics.

The contours of the midterm election were in place by the end of 2005. After the damage inflicted by Iraq, Social Security, gasoline prices, Katrina, the embarrassment of the scuttled Supreme Court nomination of Harriet Miers, and the CIA leak investigation, Bush's political profile was upside down. His approval ratings had plummeted into the 30s. Strong disapproval was almost twice as high as strong approval—and 10 percentage points higher than Clinton ever registered at the depths of his problems. Support for Iraq hit bottom once again. Bush's credibility with the public, long a pillar of his political strength, plunged. A majority of Americans no longer saw him as honest and trustworthy. His image as a strong leader, another mainstay of his public profile since 9/11, fell below 50 percent. He struggled unsuccessfully against those perceptions for most of the following year.

Beyond Iraq, Katrina did the most damage to Bush's presidency in 2005. After-action reports showed that government broke down at every level, but Washington's halting and often inept response to the disaster left a permanent mark on perceptions of the president. When the hurricane hit New Orleans, federal officials acted as if they were clueless or indifferent to the suffering and desperation that could be seen on television. Even after Bush swung into action, his normally keen instincts deserted him, particularly on his first trip to the region. White House officials were looking for a "bullhorn moment," a reprise of the president's performance atop the rubble at Ground Zero three days after the terrorist attacks, when he spontaneously put the attackers on notice that the United States was coming after them. Instead, standing next to the embattled director of the Federal Emergency Management Agency, Michael Brown, who later was fired, the president said, "Brownie, you're doing a heck of a job."

If there was one area in which Bush could claim some success, it was with his judicial nominations—despite having been defeated by a conservative revolt against his nomination of White House counsel Harriet Miers to the Supreme Court. His choice of John G. Roberts Jr., first as a replacement for Justice Sandra Day O'Connor and then, after the death of Chief Justice William Rehnquist, to become the new chief justice, drew praise from across the political spectrum and ultimately brought support from half the Democrats in the Senate. His appellate court nominations, because of an agreement among the so-called Gang of 14 to prevent both filibusters and a rules change that would bar unlimited debate for judicial nominations, broke a stalemate over a group of highly conservative and extraordinarily controversial judges. In this area Bush made good on the desire of his conservative coalition to shift the federal judiciary, including the Supreme Court, to the right.

The year 2005 ended almost as it had begun, with a successful election in Iraq in December that was marked by strong turnout even in Sunni areas that largely had boycotted earlier elections. The election came after months of pressure, cajoling, and negotiations aimed at turning the fragile democracy into a functioning government, though fears of continued violence remained high. As Iraqis prepared to vote, the president mounted the kind of political offensive not seen since the final weeks of the 2004 campaign, delivering five speeches (including a prime time address from the Oval Office), giving interviews to network anchors, meeting with members of Congress to discuss the war, and holding a press conference in a nineteen-day period that coincided with the elections.

The Bush offensive did pay some dividends politically, but they proved to be transitory. The outcome of the midterm elections was forecast many months in advance.

Looking Ahead

Bush rightly described the midterm elections as a "thumping." Republicans lost the House and the Senate. They surrendered the majority of the governorships. They lost blue states (Pennsylvania and Rhode Island) and red (Ohio, Missouri, Virginia, and Montana). They lost (narrowly) the suburbs. They lost men and women. Their margin among white men was just 4 percentage points; when they won the House in 1994 they carried white men by 26 percentage points. They lost independents by 18 points. They lost moderates by 22 points. They lost Roman Catholics, lost married women with children, and saw their margins among white evangelical Christians slip noticeably.

No one can be certain now whether the Democratic victories were an aberration or the beginning of a pendulum shift away from the Republicans. Bush still has the power to affect the terms of the 2008 election, depending on how he governs in a power-sharing arrangement—although his influence will diminish as the presidential candidates begin to occupy center stage. Democrats have yet to prove they can govern effectively enough to persuade voters to reward them with the White House or continued majorities in Congress.

The election forced immediate changes on the White House and will continue to impose more, although on Iraq there were no easy options as 2006 closed. Legislatively, Bush no longer has the luxury of governing by commandeering majorities within his party in the House and trying to force the Senate to go along. Success depends on cooperation with the Democrats. In all ways, this is not the model the president would have chosen for his final years in office.

3

George W. Bush: The Man and His Leadership

Fred I. Greenstein

A leader must be willing to listen and then be decisive enough to make a decision and stick by it. In politics, in order to lead, you've got to know what you believe. . . . You have to believe in certain values, and you must defend them at all costs. . . . You must set clear goals and convince people of those goals and constantly lead toward those goals.
GEORGE W. BUSH, MAY 25, 2002

George W. Bush entered the White House with only modest experience in public affairs and took a minimalist approach to his responsibilities before the September 11, 2001, terrorist attacks on the United States. He then began to preside with authority and assertiveness over an administration that went to great lengths to put its stamp on the national and international policy agendas but has been intensely controversial in its policies and actions. In what follows, I seek to provide a three-dimensional account of Bush the man and political leader, reviewing his early years, political rise, and presidential performance. I then analyze his political style in terms of six criteria that have proven useful for characterizing and assessing earlier chief executives—emotional intelligence, cognitive style, effectiveness as a public communicator, organizational capacity, political skill, and the extent to which he is guided by a policy vision, particularly one that is capable of attainment.[1]

Formative Years

George Walker Bush was born on July 6, 1946, in New Haven, Connecticut, where his war hero father was a Yale undergraduate.[2] In contrast to George Herbert Walker Bush, whose claim to be a Texan was belied by his Eastern accent and diffident manner, George W. Bush is very much a product of the Lone Star State. Whereas the elder Bush attended a private day school in the wealthy New York suburb of Greenwich, Connecticut, the younger Bush went to public school in Midland, Texas, where oil was the dominant economic force and the ambience was that of tract houses, Little League baseball, and easy informality. Acknowledging the difference between his Connecticut-bred father and himself, Bush has commented that while his father is mild mannered and avoids confrontation, he has the brashness and directness of a typical Texan.[3]

In 1953 the Bush family was devastated by the death of George's three-year-old sister, Robin, of leukemia. The seven-year-old George, who had no idea that his sister was gravely ill, was stunned when he was taken out of school and told that his sister was dead. His mother sank into depression. His father was frequently away from home on business, and the son sought to be his mother's consoler, playing the clown and developing the bantering manner that is one of his adult hallmarks.[4]

After completing elementary school in Texas, Bush followed his father's example and attended two intellectually rarified New England educational institutions, the elite preparatory school Phillips Academy and Yale University. He had unhappy experiences at both. At the former, he submitted a composition about the wrenching experience of learning of his sister's death but used an inappropriate word to refer to the tears he shed. He was deeply wounded when the instructor ignored the content of the paper and criticized him for the way it was written. At Yale he was offended when the college chaplain commented that his father had been defeated in his 1964 run for the Senate by "a better man." The ironic effect of Bush's exposure to these outstanding schools was to alienate him from what he came to think of as the "intellectual snobs" who set their tone.

Bush was an indifferent student at Phillips Academy and Yale, but he stood out for his social skills and popularity. In preparatory school, he became the football team's head cheerleader. At Yale he won ready admission to a fraternity that was legendary for its parties and beer consumption after revealing that he could name all of the fifty-odd fellow applicants. (None of the others could name more than a half dozen.) Bush became the group's president and won admission to Yale's most exclusive secret society, returning to Texas with friendships that were to serve him well when he ran for public office.

Bush's freshman year at Yale saw the beginning of the American military intervention in Vietnam. By his final year, the campus was wracked with anti-war protest. The political ferment of the 1960s largely passed him by, but he was far from indifferent to politics. In 1964 the eighteen-year-old Bush took part in his father's race for the Senate, delighting in the hoopla and camaraderie of campaign politics. By his mid-thirties he had worked on the campaigns of two other senatorial aspirants and participated in his father's unsuccessful campaigns for the Senate in 1970 and the Republican presidential nomination in 1980.

After Yale Bush spent two years in the Texas Air National Guard, fulfilling his military obligation. Years later when he entered politics, it was held against him that he had not chosen to volunteer for active duty in Vietnam. After completing his National Guard service, Bush attended Harvard Business School, graduating in 1974 with an MBA. He then returned to Midland, first holding an entry-level position in the oil industry and then forming an oil exploration company with funds raised through family connections. In 1978 the member of Congress in the district that included Midland announced that he was retiring, and Bush entered the race to succeed him. He won the Republican nomination but lost the general election to a conservative Democrat, who portrayed him as a carpetbagger from the Northeast and a representative of his party's moderate wing. Nevertheless, he received 47 percent of the vote in a traditionally Democratic congressional district and learned a lesson he took to heart when he reentered electoral politics—the importance of not allowing himself to be outflanked from the right.

There is another theme in Bush's early adulthood. For most of the two decades after he graduated from Yale, he was conspicuous as the under-achieving son of a super-achieving father. He drank to excess and had a devil-may-care life style that was marked by periodic alcohol-related scrapes. Gradually his life came together. In 1977 he married the level-headed librarian Laura Welch. In 1981 he became a father. During the next several years he experienced a spiritual awakening and became a regular reader of the Bible. After awakening with a fierce hangover on the morning of his fortieth birthday, he swore off alcohol, anchoring his resolve in his Christian faith.

Pre-presidential Career

Oil prices plunged in the 1980s, and Bush's company became financially untenable. Because of favorable provisions in the tax code, he was able to sell it for $2.2 million to a firm specializing in takeovers. The sale coincided with his father's efforts to become the 1988 Republican presidential nominee. Bush moved his family to Washington and became co-director with a veteran political consultant, Lee Atwater, of his father's presidential race. Bush's account of his part in the campaign highlights the importance of delegation in his managerial philosophy:

> I was a loyalty enforcer and a listening ear. When someone wanted to talk to the candidate but couldn't, I was a good substitute; people felt that if they said something to me, it would probably get to my dad. It did only if I believed it as important for him to know. A candidate needs to focus on the big picture, his message and agenda, and let others worry about most of the details.[5]

After his father's election, Bush returned to Texas where a promising business opportunity came his way. He was asked to organize an investment group to buy the Texas Rangers, a second-tier major league baseball team that had come on the market. Bush was an ideal fundraiser. He had never struck it rich in the oil business, but he had been successful in raising capital, and it did not hurt that he was the son of the president of the United States. He assembled a consortium of investors that purchased the team, naming him its managing general partner. With greater resources and new leadership, the team prospered, hiring star players and improving its competitive standing. Bush proved to be an excellent front man. He became a popular speaker at meetings of Texas business, civic, and athletic groups, and was regularly seen on television, rooting for the team from the sidelines. Before long he was a state celebrity.

Baseball was Bush's political springboard. It publicized him, demonstrated that he could manage a large organization, and gave him financial independence. After his father was defeated for reelection in 1992, Bush felt free to resume his own political career. The next year he entered the race to become the 1994 Republican opponent of Ann Richards, the state's feisty, popular Democratic governor. Assembling a highly professional campaign staff, he raised an impressive war chest and handily won his party's nomination.

Bush's next hurdle was the outspoken Richards, who had declared dismissively at the 1988 Democratic presidential nominating convention that the senior George Bush was born "with a silver foot in his mouth." Richards also derided the younger Bush, referring to him as "Shrub." Rather than replying in kind, Bush ran an issue-driven campaign. Taking as a warning his father's failure to advance a clear policy vision during his presidency, Bush ran on a small number of explicitly stated issues that already had support in the Democratically controlled legislature—greater local control of education, welfare reform, stiffer penalties for juvenile offenders, and limitations on the right to litigate against businesses. He campaigned vigorously, stayed on message, and ignored Richards's provocations, winning with 53 percent of the two-party vote.

Bush conducted his governorship in a whirl of face-to-face persuasion and negotiation. Even before the election results were in, he forged a bond with the legislature's most influential Democrat. On taking office, he formally proposed the program on which he had campaigned. By the end of the first legislative session, he had advanced that program in dozens of meetings with lawmakers of both parties. All four of his signature measures were enacted. Although he had gone along with compromises in their provisions, Bush declared victory and ran for a second term in 1998.[6] He was reelected with a record 69 percent of the vote, drawing support from such traditionally Democratic groups as women and minorities.

As governor, Bush was sweeping in his acts of delegation. A study of his schedule found that when a report was delivered to him on a tragedy in which a number of Texas college students had died in a bonfire, he read neither the report nor its executive summary, leaving it to his aides to highlight a few paragraphs of its conclusions. Even in the sensitive realm of capital punishment,

Bush relied heavily on the recommendations of his aides, reducing the time he spent on reviews of death sentences from thirty to fifteen minutes in the course of his governorship. There was a laid-back quality to his management of his time as governor, including an extended mid-day break during which he worked out and had lunch.[7] It was by no means obvious from his gubernatorial style that he was burning to seek the presidency.

To the White House

As the 2000 season for selecting presidential nominees approached, it was evident that the Republican Party needed a strong candidate if it was not to be defeated as it was in 1992 and 1996. Bush's name recognition as the son of a former president and his gubernatorial record made him an instant front-runner, a status that enabled him to raise an unprecedented $90 million in campaign funds. In February, Bush suffered a stinging blow in New Hampshire, where Republican voters chose Arizona senator John McCain over him to be the party's nominee. But he rebounded, clinching the nomination in March with victories in California, New York, and seven other states. Vice President Al Gore locked in the Democratic nomination the same week, and the two men girded themselves for the presidential campaign.

As he had in Texas, Bush took pains to enunciate an explicit policy agenda. In doing so he followed the precept he states in his campaign autobiography, that "the first challenge of leadership . . . is to outline a clear vision and agenda."[8] Included in his program were proposals for sharply reduced taxes, military modernization, Social Security and health reform, and measures intended to improve the circumstances of disadvantaged groups that fell under what he referred to as the "compassionate" side of his conservatism. An example of the latter was a testing-based educational program designed to identify schools in which students were failing to learn basic skills and provide their students with resources to attend better schools.[9]

Nothing Bush said in the campaign anticipated his administration's military involvements in Afghanistan and Iraq and its commitment to rebuild those nations. Indeed, he declared his opposition to a globally expansive foreign policy, criticizing the use of the American military in "nation building." The danger of an activist foreign policy, he asserted, was that the United States would be disliked for its arrogance, whereas "if we are a humble nation, they'll welcome us."[10]

The content of Bush's program seemed beside the point to many political observers. It appeared likely that he would be defeated by Gore, who represented the incumbent administration in a period of prosperity, had more governmental experience than Bush, and had the reputation of being a formidable debater. But the economy began to sag, Bush held his own in the presidential debates, and Gore ran an unimpressive campaign. As election day approached, the polls showed Bush and Gore running neck and neck. What ensued was one of the closest and most controversial election outcomes in the nation's history. Gore ran ahead in the popular vote by a fraction of 1 percent, and there was a close division in the electoral vote.

The outcome of the election hinged on the Florida electoral vote. Bush and Gore were in a dead heat in the state's popular vote, and there was a bewildering array of controversies about alleged flaws in the mechanics of voting in various localities. There followed a thirty-six-day impasse over the Florida vote count, which was broken by a five-to-four ruling of the United States Supreme Court that had the effect of awarding Bush the Florida electoral vote, making him the winner. On the evening of December 13, Gore conceded. Within the hour, Bush made his victory speech, doing so in the chamber of the Texas House of Representatives. He had chosen that venue, he explained, "because it has been home to bipartisan cooperation," adding that "the spirit of cooperation we have seen in this hall is what is needed in Washington, D.C."[11]

A Bland Beginning

Given the controversial conclusion to the 2000 presidential campaign, Bush might have been expected to assume the presidency in a firestorm of contention. In fact, the political system's healing processes had set in. The media coverage of Bush's inauguration focused on the dignified pomp of the occasion, not the legitimacy of the process that led up to it. Bush seemed at ease as he took the oath of office, and the fourteen-minute inaugural address written by his talented speech writer, Michael Gerson, was free of apologetics.

The address was widely praised for its eloquence. Taking its theme from Bush's campaign references to "compassion," it declared that "the ambitions of many Americans are limited by failing schools and hidden prejudice and the circumstances of their birth" and promised to "reclaim America's schools, before ignorance and apathy claim more young lives." The speech enumerated the issues on which Bush campaigned and quoted a rhetorical question asked of Thomas Jefferson by one of his contemporaries during the dark days of the American Revolution: "Do you not think an angel rides in the whirlwind and directs this storm?" The address concluded by repeating the figure of speech and affirming that it continued to apply to the contemporary United States.

The effect of the address's poetic imagery was blunted by Bush's prosaic delivery, however, and further weakened by his propensity to pause in mid-phrase and stumble over words. By the time he arrived at the address's moving peroration, his halting presentation made it obvious that he was reading a script rather than speaking in a voice that was natural to him. Bush was more fluent on unscripted occasions, but then there was the risk that his lack of experience would lead him to misspeak, as he did in an April 26 interview in which he stated that the United States was committed to do "whatever it takes" to defend Taiwan from attack by China. In fact, it had long been American policy to remain vague about how to respond to such a contingency, and Bush had not intended to signal a policy departure. The State Department was compelled to engage in damage control, saying that Bush had only meant to highlight the seriousness with which the United States took its relationship with Taiwan.[12]

There was another problem with Bush's early public communications—their infrequency. Bush never addressed the nation from the Oval Office until the evening of September 11, 2001. He never convened a full-fledged, prime-time news conference until a month later. He periodically fielded questions from reporters, but did so in hastily convened exchanges, avoiding pre-announced conferences in which he would have had to face media heavyweights. Bush also put little emphasis on his capacity as the nation's symbolic leader. Thus, he made no statement to the nation when Cincinnati was wracked with racial unrest, and he did not join in the welcoming ceremony for the crew of a reconnaissance plane that had been held captive in China for eleven days. Three months into the Bush presidency the *Washington Post*'s David Broder devoted a column to Bush's neglect of the bully pulpit, saying that the American people had been left without a "clear definition of their new leader."[13]

Yet in other respects Bush exhibited conspicuous strengths—for instance, in organizing his presidency and pursuing his legislative agenda. He made his most significant organizational choice even before the Republican convention anointed him as his party's official nominee, selecting as his running mate the Washington-wise Dick Cheney, who compensated for his own lack of national experience. With Cheney as a source of advice, Bush appointed an experienced White House staff and cabinet, not waiting until the resolution of the Florida electoral dispute to engage in transition planning.

Bush's appointees included veterans of the Gerald Ford, Ronald Reagan, and first Bush presidencies, and two of his longtime Texas aides, political strategist Karl Rove and communications adviser Karen Hughes. His national security team was particularly well seasoned: Secretary of State Colin Powell had been national security adviser and chairman of the Joint Chiefs of Staff, Secretary of Defense Donald Rumsfeld had been defense secretary in the Ford administration, and National Security Adviser Condoleezza Rice had been an important foreign policy aide in his father's White House.[14]

Bush had notable successes in advancing his agenda, not only by practicing the bipartisanship he lauded in his victory speech, but also by rigorous partisanship. Bipartisanship was evident in the enactment of the administration's testing-based education bill, which was hammered out in meetings with legislators of both parties, including the most prominent congressional liberal, Massachusetts Democrat Edward M. Kennedy. Congress enacted the measure by the end of the year. But partisanship was the order of the day when Bush mobilized an overwhelming majority of congressional Republicans and a handful of Democrats to enact his administration's record tax cut. Four months into his presidency, however, the partisanship boomeranged. The administration's allies on Capitol Hill had sought to punish the moderate Republican Vermont senator, James Jeffords, who had voted for a smaller tax reduction than Bush had proposed, by eliminating a program that was vital to his state's dairy industry. On May 24 Jeffords resigned from his party, placing the Democrats in control of the Senate.[15]

By September 11 there had been signs that Bush was growing in the job. In the episode in which an American reconnaissance aircraft was forced down by China, for example, his first response had been to issue a peremptory demand that the plane be returned and the crew released, but he backed off and remained patient while negotiations went on to release the crew. And in August he gave a thoughtful address to the nation on the controversial issue of government funding of embryonic stem cell research, making it evident that he had begun to recognize the centrality of public communication to presidential leadership. Still there was a widespread view in the political community that he was over his head in the nation's highest office.

Terror and Transformation

Bush was visiting a Florida elementary school to promote his administration's education bill the morning of September 11 when he was informed that an airliner had crashed into the north tower of the World Trade Center. When a second airliner flew into the south tower fifteen minutes later, it became evident that the first collision had been no accident. By mid-morning, both towers of the World Trade Center had collapsed, a third plane had crashed into the Pentagon, and a fourth into a Pennsylvania field. Before leaving the school Bush read a statement declaring that "terrorism against our nation will not stand."

Because of concern that Bush would be a target of terrorists, he was flown to an Air Force base in Louisiana, where he made another public statement, and then to the control center of the Strategic Air Command in Nebraska, where he presided electronically over a meeting of the National Security Council (NSC). The director of the Central Intelligence Agency informed the NSC that the attacks were almost certainly the work of al Qaeda, an Afghanistan-based organization that had been responsible for other acts of terrorism directed at the United States. Bush then returned to the White House, where he addressed the nation from the Oval Office, asserting that the attacks were "acts of war," that there "would be a monumental struggle between good and evil" in which "good will prevail," and that the United States would "make no distinction between the terrorists who committed these acts and those who harbor them."

During the chaotic day of the attack, Bush gave the appearance of being less than completely self-assured. He read his statements from Florida and Louisiana mechanically and did not seem fully at ease as he delivered his September 11 address to the nation. He then underwent a striking transformation. On September 14 he delivered a deeply emotional tribute to the victims of the terrorist attacks at a memorial service at Washington's National Cathedral. After the service he went to New York City, where he inspected the wreckage of the World Trade Center, using a bullhorn to address the rescue workers. When members of the audience shouted that they could not hear him, Bush replied, "I can hear you. The rest of the world hears you, and the people who knocked these buildings down will hear all of us soon!"

In the weeks that followed, Bush became a compelling public presence. On September 20 he made a forceful presentation to Congress, giving the Taliban regime in Afghanistan an ultimatum to turn the al Qaeda leadership over to the United States and close its terrorist camps. Three weeks later he gave a similarly strong address to the United Nations. Most impressive was his October 11 prime-time news conference in the East Room of the White House. He responded in depth to questions, radiating a sense of composure and displaying a thorough comprehension of what his administration had begun to refer to as the "war on terror."

There was almost an immediate surge in the public's ratings of Bush's job performance. In a Gallup survey fielded the week before the terrorist attacks, his approval level was at low ebb for the first eight months of his presidency—51 percent. Two weeks later it had soared to 90 percent, the record high in a half century of Gallup presidential approval ratings.[16] Members of the political community also formed markedly more positive views of Bush's leadership qualities. Before September 11, even many of his supporters had been persuaded that he was not up to his responsibilities. Thereafter even many of his critics concluded that he had been underestimated, a view that extended to other nations. On October 20, for example, a columnist for Germany's influential *Frankfurter Allgemeine* commented that Bush had grown into his job "before our eyes," comparing him to another president who rose to the challenge of his responsibilities following an inauspicious beginning—Harry S. Truman.[17]

One reason Bush improved his mastery of policy in the weeks following September 11 was the depth of his immersion in deliberations. In the month between the bombings of the World Trade Center and the Pentagon and his bravura October 11 press conference, Bush met with his NSC twenty-four times in meetings that were far from pro forma. In the September 12 meeting, for example, there was a sharp debate that foreshadowed the 2003 military intervention in Iraq. Vice President Cheney and Defense Secretary Rumsfeld advocated attacking not just al Qaeda but also nations that sponsor terrorism, notably Iraq. Secretary of State Colin Powell disagreed, arguing that the American people readily would back action against the terrorists linked to 9/11 but would be puzzled by a proposal to attack Iraq. Bush halted the debate, indicating that this was not the time to resolve that issue.[18]

In early October the Afghan regime let it be known that it would not surrender the al Qaeda leadership, and the United States and its ally, Great Britain, began an intensive bombing campaign. Later in the month U.S. Special Forces entered Afghanistan and supported the anti-Taliban Northern Alliance. By November 13 the Northern Alliance had occupied the Afghan capital of Kabul, and in early December, the last major Taliban stronghold surrendered. When the Gallup organization polled the public at the end of December, Bush's approval level was a towering 86 percent.

Iraq and Beyond

Bush had postponed a decision on whether to target Iraq in the War on Terror in the September 12, 2001, NSC meeting, but Iraq came into his cross-hairs in his January 2002 State of the Union address. Anticipating the doctrine of preemption that his administration would formally promulgate later in the year, Bush declared that he would not "wait on events" while "the world's most dangerous weapons" were acquired by "the world's most dangerous regimes." One such regime, he specified, was Iraq, which he grouped with Iran and North Korea in what he described as an "axis of evil."

Bush's assertion sent shock waves. Whereas his response to September 11 had been favorably received, there was widespread criticism of his "axis of evil" locution. Some of it was prompted by a belief that Bush had lumped together nations that differed in the threats that they posed and some was directed at the use of the word "evil," which led critics to worry about whether his commitment to evangelical Christianity was leading him to advance an inappropriately moralistic foreign policy. Bush's address presaged a major preoccupation of the second and third years of his first term—his efforts to come to terms with Iraq.

The Bush administration embarked on a procession of actions directed at Saddam Hussein's regime. Diplomacy prevailed in the fall of 2002, when the United States persuaded the United Nations Security Council to enact a resolution insisting that Iraq destroy any weapons of mass destruction it might have and admit UN inspectors to its territory to ensure that it had done so. Early in 2003, however, the administration called for military action. It attempted to persuade the Security Council to authorize the use of force on the grounds that Iraq had failed to comply with the UN demand for effective inspections. When it became evident that UN support would not be forthcoming, the Bush administration, with Britain as its principal ally, embarked on an invasion of Iraq.

The assault began on March 20, 2003. American troops took possession of Baghdad on April 6. On May 1 Bush dramatically landed on an aircraft carrier from which he made a triumphant speech, declaring the end of "major combat operations." He had spoken too soon. The chaotic situation following the fall of Saddam Hussein spawned a tenacious insurgency that continued into Bush's second term. As the American death toll in Iraq mounted, Bush's poll ratings eroded. In 2004 he faced the unenviable prospect of running for reelection with only a modest level of public support. Surveys showed that he was widely respected for the firmness of his leadership but that there was declining acceptance of his administration's actions in Iraq. Bush's approval level hovered around 50 percent throughout the year, an unpromising level for a chief executive seeking reelection.

The Democrats nominated three-term Massachusetts senator John Kerry to run against Bush in 2004. Kerry was widely viewed as a formidable contender. While he had not been responsible for major legislative initiatives during his years in Congress, Kerry's service on Capitol Hill had been marked by a willingness to dig tenaciously into important problems. He had, for example, allied himself with fellow Vietnam War veteran John McCain in a searching investigation that put to rest the view that American prisoners remained in Vietnam. This opened the way for the United States to establish diplomatic relations with its former adversaries in Hanoi. The very fact that Kerry had served in Vietnam appeared to be in his favor at a time when the nation was engaged in a Vietnam-like war in the Middle East. Moreover, he had placed himself in harm's way, winning decorations for valor in combat before leaving the military and becoming a critic of the war.

Kerry, however, proved to have a proclivity for convoluted verbal constructions and a flat speaking style, whereas Bush made effective use of Texas vernacular to reiterate his policy positions, and his delivery was punchy and incisive. Kerry's campaign also suffered because his team was slow to reply to the relentlessly negative characterizations of him by the Bush camp, which accused him of "flip-flopping" on issues and turned his Vietnam-era experience against him by alleging that his antiwar protests had demoralized American troops in Vietnam. As in 2000, the vote was closely divided in 2004, but this time Bush won the popular vote, albeit with a 50.7 percent majority.[19] As Gary C. Jacobson has shown, the narrowness of Bush's victory reflects the sharpest polarization of the electorate in the half century of American public opinion polling.[20]

Second-term Ambitions and Realities

It was a favorable harbinger for Bush's second-term program that his party maintained control of Congress, slightly increasing its majorities in both chambers. But it did not bode well that the margin of victory was the closest for an incumbent president in American history and that he failed to get the bounce in public support that often accrues to a presidential winner. A national survey conducted by the *Washington Post* two weeks after the election found Bush's approval level to be a mere 50 percent. Moreover, of the 48 percent of the public expressing disapproval, there was a hard core of 38 percent that voiced strong disapproval.[21]

Bush was unfazed. Two days after the election, he convened a press conference in which he declared that he had won "political capital" with his victory and intended to spend it, adding that seeking to shape public policy "is my style." Asserting that he would use that capital "for what I told the people I would spend it on," Bush reiterated his campaign proposals, which included limitations on the ability of debtors to declare bankruptcy and on "irresponsible" class action lawsuits, the extension of his administration's school testing program to high schools, simplification of the tax code, and a controversial proposal to permit younger workers to divert a portion of their Social Security taxes to personal accounts that would be invested in the stock market. In addition to setting forth an ambitious domestic program, Bush let it be known that he was determined to continue the military involvement in Iraq until it was strong enough to defend itself.

Meanwhile, the process of personnel change that marks the later years of most administrations, especially two-term presidencies, was under way. Within two weeks after Bush's reelection, seven cabinet heads announced their resignations, the most notable of them being Attorney General John Ashcroft and Secretary of State Colin Powell. Bush replaced both with members of his staff with whom he had close personal ties, White House counsel Alberto R. Gonzales for Ashcroft and Condoleezza Rice for Powell. Within the first eighteen months of Bush's second term there were to be twelve resignations of cabinet members, all but one of whom had been replaced. Pointedly, however, Bush chose not to replace Secretary of Defense Rumsfeld, although he was deeply controversial as the architect of the administration's much criticized conduct of the war.

The opening months of Bush's second term witnessed three administration legislative victories. Congress quickly enacted the measures relating to bankruptcy and class action lawsuits. It also granted the administration's request for a multibillion-dollar appropriation for the war in Iraq. Bush concentrated his own efforts on the Social Security proposal, promoting it in numerous speeches and town hall forums. Congress failed to act on the measure, which met strong opposition from senior citizen advocacy groups. Still, the lawmakers did approve Bush's energy and transportation bills, as well as an administration-sponsored Central American trade agreement, before adjourning for summer recess.[22]

On August 2, 2005, Bush departed for a month-long vacation in Texas with reason to be pleased with the success of his program so far, but by the time he returned to Washington, there had been a dramatic turn for the worse in his political standing. In the final week of August, a catastrophic hurricane devastated the coastal communities of Mississippi and flooded much of New Orleans, taking more than 1,800 lives. Bush was subjected to criticism from Republicans as well as Democrats for being slow to recognize the magnitude of the disaster and for the government's fumbling relief effort. On August 31 Bush ended his vacation and returned to Washington to engage in crisis management, but by then his reputation as a can-do president was much diminished.

There were two major nonlegislative developments during the first year of Bush's second term: a further drop in his already modest public support and events related to Supreme Court vacancies. As the military commitment in Iraq persisted, the casualty toll mounted, as did public discontent with Bush. By June 2005, his ratings had declined to the point at which disapproval of his job performance exceeded approval, a negative ratio that continued in 2006.[23]

The composition of the Supreme Court had remained constant for over a decade when Bush began his new term. Because two of the justices were over 80 and a third was over 70, it was probable that there would be vacancies on his watch. That probability became a certainty in July when Justice Sandra Day O'Connor announced that she intended to retire. O'Connor's replacement was of great significance because she had often cast the deciding vote on the closely divided court, alternating between its liberal and conservative blocs. Bush nominated as her successor John G. Roberts Jr., a federal appeals court judge with conservative political leanings and outstanding legal credentials. Roberts had only been on the bench for four years, but he had argued numerous cases before the high court as a member of the George H. W. Bush Justice Department and in private practice. Roberts's testimony in his Senate confirmation hearings was erudite, polished, and incisive, reflecting favorably on Bush's judgment in nominating him.

Early in September, a second vacancy was created by the death of Supreme Court Chief Justice William H. Rehnquist. Moving rapidly, Bush proposed that Roberts succeed Rehnquist as chief justice rather than replace O'Connor. Roberts was confirmed within the month. It remained for Bush to nominate O'Connor's successor. His first choice, White House counsel Harriet Miers, failed to pass muster with Republican conservatives and she withdrew. Bush then nominated federal appeals judge Samuel Alito Jr., a jurist with an impressive legal record and a favorite of Republican conservatives. Alito's confirmation testimony was clear and well informed, and his diffident manner belied efforts to depict him as a right-wing extremist. He was confirmed on January 31, the day Bush delivered his 2006 State of the Union message.

The Roberts and Alito appointments provided welcome relief to an increasingly beleaguered Bush White House. In the final months of 2005, Bush's approval ratings declined to new lows, and Bush was rebuffed when what the *Washington Post* referred to as a "newly emboldened Congress" took two actions that he opposed. It amended a military appropriations bill to forbid the use of harsh interrogation procedures on detainees and refused Bush's request to extend an act passed after 9/11 that provided for new presidential powers to combat terrorism, insisting that it be modified to protect civil liberties.[24]

Bush's 2006 State of the Union address, which was notably lacking in bold proposals, reflected a pragmatic recognition of what a politically weakened president can accomplish in an election year. The policies he did propose had a distinctly centrist cast. They included a program to enhance the nation's competitiveness in the global economy by training high school teachers in advanced mathematics and science and a proposal intended to reduce the nation's reliance on oil imports by developing alternative energy sources. Rather than urge passage of the previous year's tax and Social Security proposals, Bush called for the creation of a bipartisan commission to study these matters.

Pragmatism ruled the day in other areas of Bush's sixth-year program. Domestically he advanced a position on immigration reform that fell between the stances of agricultural and commercial interests that needed immigrant labor and conservative opponents of illegal immigration. Internationally, his administration began to emphasize diplomacy rather than military preemption. Although Iran and North Korea appeared to be developing nuclear weapons, Bush was measured in his rhetoric, making such assertions as "these problems didn't arise overnight, and they don't get solved overnight."[25] Even in trimming his sails, however, Bush made evident his continuing determination to leave an imprint on the nation's policies.

Despite setting modest goals, Bush found himself increasingly mired in what the political scientist John Mueller refers to as "the Iraq syndrome"—a pattern in which the steady increase in American casualties in Iraq has been paralleled by a steady decrease in public approval of the president's job performance.[26] This dynamic was particularly evident in the final month of 2006, when the death toll in Iraq reached 3,000 and approval of Bush in a *Washington Post* poll sank to a near low of 36 percent.[27]

Bush's unpopularity had inevitable consequences for the 2006 midterm election: the Democrats won control of both houses of Congress for the first time since 1992. When the results were in, Bush acknowledged that his party had taken a "thumping" and announced that he was accepting the resignation of Secretary of Defense Rumsfeld in order to bring "fresh perspective" to his administration's handling of Iraq.[28] One such perspective became available early in December in the long-awaited report of the bipartisan Iraq Study Group, which was co-chaired by the senior Bush's secretary of state, James Baker III, and a respected former member of Congress, Lee Hamilton. The report, which was scathing in its implications for the administration's policies in Iraq, declared that the "situation in Iraq is grave and deteriorating" and proposed that the nation's defense be turned over to its own forces by 2008.[29]

It remains to be seen how Bush might respond to such advice and to his changed circumstances more generally. As the seventh year of his presidency began, he sent mixed signals. On the one hand, he rejected the implicit exit strategy in the report of the Iraq Study Group, announcing that some 20,000 additional troops would be sent to Iraq with the aim of helping the Iraqis pacify Baghdad.[30] On the other hand, he reached out to the Democrats on domestic policy, visiting the annual retreat of House Democrats and making proposals on key domestic issues.[31] Of the possible scenarios for the remainder of Bush's time in the White House, one might resemble the final years of the Woodrow Wilson presidency, when an unbending chief executive refused to negotiate with those who disagreed with him and suffered a crushing defeat. A second quite different possibility might parallel the reversal of direction of Ronald Reagan, who in his first term castigated the Soviet Union as an "Evil Empire," but in his second term entered into a highly successful peacemaking process with that nation.

The Elements of a Political Style

It remains to characterize Bush's leadership style in terms of the criteria introduced in the opening paragraph of this chapter.

EMOTIONAL INTELLIGENCE

No quality is more vital than emotional intelligence in the custodian of the most potentially lethal military force in human history. To be emotionally intelligent a president need not be a paragon of mental health. What is critical is that his (and someday her) public actions not be distorted by uncontrolled passions. Franklin D. Roosevelt, for example, left much to be desired as husband and father, but there was a superb fit between his emotions and the demands he faced as president.

By the litmus of emotional intelligence, the heavy-drinking young George W. Bush was too volatile to be entrusted with a responsible public position, particularly that of American president in the nuclear age. It would not be surprising if a man who abused alcohol until early middle age and abruptly went on the wagon proved to be an emotional tinder box. However, Bush's performance as a businessman and as governor of Texas was not marred by emotional excesses; he weathered his setback in New Hampshire in the 2000 campaign with seeming equanimity; and he seemed almost chipper in the face of the steady decline of his public support in his second term.

Most important, Bush appears not to have been dominated by his emotions in the two major national security crises that marked his first term, those in Afghanistan and Iraq. The best account of the former is Bob Woodward's in-depth report of the Bush administration's decisionmaking in the months immediately after September 11. Woodward, who is famed for his access to inside sources, does not report a single instance in which Bush acted on uncontrolled impulse. Indeed, Bush exhibited noteworthy insight into his own emotional makeup, explaining to Woodward that it was in his nature to be "fiery" in the sense of being eager to act on problems as soon as they arose. Recognizing that the conditions for action might not be ripe, he had made it part of National Security Adviser Rice's job to "take the edge off" such impulses, he explained, adding, "she's good at that."[32]

COGNITIVE STYLE

Bush's strong performance in his exchanges with the press after 9/11 refutes the implication of his critics that he is deficient in native intelligence. He periodically revealed himself to be ill-informed in the early months of his presidency, but once his mind was concentrated by the attacks on New York and Washington, there was a sharp improvement in the extent of his political information, a development that was attested to by members of Congress who were in regular contact with him. As one of them put it, "He's as smart as he wants to be."[33]

It is possible, however, to be knowledgeable without being well equipped to reason about the complex tradeoffs a president must address. Bush is better at enunciating the broad outlines of his administration's positions than elucidating the subtleties of their pros and cons. In this he contrasts with a leader with whom he has periodically shared a podium, British prime minister Tony Blair. At a March 25, 2003, joint meeting with the press, for example, Bush and Blair responded to questions about how long the fighting in Iraq would continue. Blair was expansive and analytic, reviewing the roots of the conflict, its global ramifications, and its likely aftermath, whereas Bush contented himself with such laconic assertions as "however long it takes."[34]

Bush's mastery of the cognitive demands of presidential leadership is also a function of his management style. As a former corporate chief executive officer and the product of a business school, he relies heavily on his staff to provide the background for the actions he takes. This contrasts with President John F. Kennedy, who kept his top subordinates on their toes by personally reaching down into the federal bureaucracy to consult with subject matter specialists. One instance in which Bush might have profited from a more hands-on approach to informing himself was in preparing for the 2003 State of the Union address in which he made the unqualified—and inaccurate—claim that Iraq possessed weapons of mass destruction and was seeking to develop nuclear weapons. If he were more personally engaged in establishing the factual basis of his policies, he likely would be less prone to such errors.

EFFECTIVENESS AS A PUBLIC COMMUNICATOR

In his early months in the White House, Bush seemed not to recognize the rhetorical potentialities of the presidency. He was silent on occasions when there was a need for him to be heard; he delivered prepared texts mechanically and unpersuasively; and when he was unscripted, he risked misspeaking. For all of his improvement as a public communicator after 9/11, Bush continues to lack the easy fluency of an FDR, Kennedy, or Reagan. His speeches are most likely to be effective when he has taken part in their preparation and takes the time to rehearse, as was the case with the 2006 State of the Union address. When that does not occur, Bush is capable of reverting to a labored mode of presentation, even when the stakes are high.

ORGANIZATIONAL CAPACITY

It speaks well for Bush's organizational capacity that he launched his presidency with an impressively seasoned team, but how he has managed his associates is a quite different matter. There has been a succession of instructive writings by investigative journalists on the inner working of the Bush administration, especially with respect to Iraq. Included are a series of reconstructions of the administration's decisionmaking by Bob Woodward and a biography of Colin Powell by Karen DeYoung, which draws on extensive interviews with the former secretary of state.[35] While these works differ in their specifics, they are strikingly alike in their accounts of flawed policies and a dysfunctional policymaking process.

The policy flaws began with the decision to invade Iraq, which never was thoroughly debated. They continued with the invasion itself, which was carried out with too small a force to secure the nation. Another problematic early decision was the disbanding of Iraqi armed forces, which provided the motivation and manpower for an instant insurgency. Underlying the specific blunders was a larger failure to take account of the fractiousness of Iraqi society.

These policies emerged from an unsystematic, ideologically driven decisionmaking process in which back-channeling was the order of the day, and the hawkish vice president and secretary of defense regularly succeeded in marginalizing the secretary of state. The Bush administration's policymaking turned on its head the common prescription that important decisions should be based on sharply joined debate in which alternative points of view are argued before the chief executive. The administration's approach could scarcely have been a greater contrast with the approach favored by the most organizationally proficient modern president—Dwight D. Eisenhower. "I know of one way in which you can be sure you have done your best to make a wise decision," the former supreme allied commander once remarked. "That is to get the responsible policy makers with their different viewpoints in front of you, and listen to them debate. I do not believe in bringing them in one at a time, and therefore being more impressed by the most recent one you hear than the earlier ones."[36]

POLITICAL SKILL

The congenitally gregarious George W. Bush resembles his fellow Texan Lyndon B. Johnson in his aptitude for personal politics. Both in Texas and in Washington, Bush has demonstrated his ability to work effectively on both sides of the aisle, but he has displayed a hard-edged partisanship in Washington that was not evident in his home state. Nevertheless, whether by forming cross-party coalitions or mobilizing congressional Republicans, Bush has been remarkably successful in bringing about the enactment of his program. But there is a sense that his political skill is more tactical than strategic—that is, he has been better at getting short-term results than advancing long-term interests. Thus, despite billing himself in the 2000 campaign as a "uniter not a divider," the polarization of the American political system has reached a new high on his watch, and his administration's foreign policy has contributed to an anti-Americanism that cannot be in the nation's interest.[37]

POLICY VISION

The senior George Bush was famously indifferent to what he dismissed as "the vision thing." The younger Bush has faulted his father for failing to enunciate a policy agenda and not building on the popularity he accrued from the American victory in the 1991 Gulf war for his reelection campaign. George W. Bush is endowed with a policy vision, one that results from his commitment to his administration's program and his conviction that if he fails to set his own agenda, others will set it for him. However, there is a paradox to his policy-driven leadership. Bush's persistence in advancing a program is a source of political strength, but he has the weakness of that strength—a tendency to overload the policymaking process and pursue his program to the point of diminishing returns. And by virtue of having a policy vision, he runs the risk of having a defective vision—of advancing policies that are not attainable or that are even counterproductive.

Notes

1. For an elaboration on these criteria see the first and last chapters of Fred I. Greenstein, *The Presidential Difference: Leadership Style from FDR to George W. Bush,* 2d ed. (Princeton University Press, 2004). In what follows, I build on the discussion of George W. Bush in that work. On the meaning of the psychological construct "emotional intelligence," see Daniel Goleman, *Emotional Intelligence* (New York: Bantam Books, 1995).

2. The most balanced biography of George W. Bush is by Bill Minutaglio, *First Son: George W. Bush and the Bush Family Dynasty* (New York: Times Books, 1999). See also Elizabeth Mitchell, *W: Revenge of the Bush Dynasty* (New York: Hyperion, 2000). During the 2000 presidential campaign there were a number of useful journalistic accounts of Bush's life. One of the best is the *Washington Post* series, "The Life and Times of George W. Bush," which appeared in July 2000.

3. George W. Bush, *A Charge to Keep: My Journey to the White House* (New York: HarperCollins, 1999), p. 182.

4. A manner that is engagingly captured in the 2002 HBO documentary *Journeys with George,* which documents the campaign trail

antics of candidate Bush and the reporters covering his race for the presidency.

5. Bush, *A Charge to Keep,* p. 180.

6. Minutaglio, *First Son,* pp. 295–303.

7. Alan C. Miller and Judy Pasternak, "Records Show Bush's Focus on Big Picture," *Los Angeles Times,* August 2, 2000.

8. Bush, *A Charge to Keep,* p. 97.

9. For a Bush adviser's elaboration, see Marvin Olasky, *Compassionate Conservatism: What It Is, What It Does, and How It Can Transform America* (New York: Free Press, 2000).

10. Commission on Presidential Debates, "Second Bush-Gore Presidential Debate," October 11, 2000, www.debates.org/pages/debhis2000.html.

11. "Bush's Remarks on the End of the Race," *New York Times,* December 14, 2000.

12. For a succinct summary of this event, see *Facts on File World News Digest Yearbook, 2001* (New York: Facts on File News Services, 2002), p. 304.

13. David S. Broder, "The Reticent President," *Washington Post,* April 22, 2001.

14. John P. Burke, *Becoming President: The Bush Transition, 2000–2004* (Boulder, Colo.: Lynne Rienner, 2004).

15. John C. Fortier and Norman J. Ornstein, "President Bush: Legislative Strategist," in *The George W. Bush Presidency: An Early Assessment,* edited by Fred I. Greenstein (Johns Hopkins University Press, 2003), pp. 138–72.

16. Richard A. Brody, "President Bush and the Public," in *The George W. Bush Presidency,* edited by Greenstein, pp. 228–44.

17. Leo Weiland, "Bush's New Image," *Frankfurter Allgemeine* (English language edition), October 20, 2001.

18. A list of the post–September 11 NSC meetings can be found in the index of Bob Woodward's *Bush at War* (New York: Simon & Schuster, 2002), p. 367; the exchange between Rumsfeld and Powell appears on p. 49. Bush was also immersed in information during the Iraq war, receiving

as much as three hours a day of briefings. See Elisabeth Bumiller, "President, No Matter Where, Keeps Battlefield Close," *New York Times,* March 30, 2003. See also Judy Keene and Laurence McQuillan, "Bush Dives into Details of Iraq Conflict," *USA Today,* March 21, 2003.

19. Bush received 286 electoral votes to Kerry's 251. If the closely divided state of Ohio had gone Democratic, the outcome would have been a mirror image of 2000, with the Democrats loosing the popular vote but winning the election in the Electoral College.

20. Gary C. Jacobson, *A Divider, Not a Uniter: George W. Bush and the American People* (New York: Pearson Longman, 2007).

21. PollingReport.com, www.pollingreport.com/.

22. Richard W. Stevenson, "Despite Problems, Bush Continues to Make Advances on His Agenda," *New York Times,* June 29, 2005.

23. PollingReport.com, www.pollingreport.com/BushJob.htm.

24. Jim VandeHei and Charles Babington, "Newly Emboldened Congress had Dogged Bush This Year," *Washington Post,* December 23, 2005.

25. Jim VandeHei and Jonathan Weisman, "On Immigration, Bush Seeks 'Middle Ground,'" *Washington Post,* May 16, 2006; David E. Sanger, "Bush's Shift: Being Patient with Foes," *New York Times,* July 10, 2006.

26. John Mueller, "The Iraq Syndrome," *Foreign Affairs,* November-December 2005, pp. 44–54.

27. Casualties in Iraq are reported in www.icasualties.com. Bush's approval level is reported in www.pollingreport.com.

28. "Bush Replaces Rumsfeld to Get 'Fresh Perspective,'" November 9, 2006, CNN.com.

29. The Iraq Study Group report can be found at the website of the US Institute of Peace: www.usip.org/isg/.

30. George W. Bush, "Address to the Nation," Office of the Press Secretary, White House, January 10, 2007.

31. Michael Abramowitz and Paul Kane, "At Democratic Meeting, Bush Appeals for Cooperation," *Washington Post,* February 1, 2007.

32. Woodward, *Bush at War,* p. 158.

33. Stephen Thomma, "Growing on the Job," *Miami Herald,* December 9, 2001.

34. White House, "President Bush, Prime Minister Blair Hold Press Availability," March 27, 2003 (www.whitehouse.gov/news/releases/2003/03/20030327-3.html).

35. Bob Woodward, *Bush at War* (2002), *Plan of Attack* (New York: Simon & Schuster, 2004), and *State of Denial: Bush at War Part III* (New York: Simon & Schuster, 2006), and Karen DeYoung, *Soldier: The Life of Colin Powell* (New York: Knopf, 2006). For a wide-ranging review of writings on the relationship between the organization of the Bush administration and its Iraq policy, see John P. Burke, "From Success to Failure? Iraq and the Organization of George W. Bush's Decision Making," in *The Polarized Presidency of George W. Bush*, edited by George C. Edwards III and Desmond S. King (Oxford University Press, forthcoming 2007).

36. Dwight D. Eisenhower, Columbia University Oral History Interview, July 20, 1967, uncorrected transcript. The last sentence of the quotation was unaccountably omitted in the corrected final transcript. The classical statement of the importance of rigorous debate in presidential advisory systems is Alexander L. George, "The Case for Multiple Advocacy in Making Foreign Policy," *American Political Science Review* 66 (1972), pp. 751–85. On Eisenhower's institutional procedures for fostering such debate, see Fred I. Greenstein and Richard H. Immerman, "Effective National Security Advising: Recovering the Eisenhower Legacy," *Political Science Quarterly* 115 (2000), pp. 335–45.

37. Gary C. Jacobson, *A Divider, Not a Uniter; Global Opinion: The Spread of Anti-Americanism* (Washington, D.C.: Pew Global Attitudes Project, Pew Research Center, January 24, 2005).

4

Bush Foreign Policy: First-Term Choices, Second-Term Consequences

David E. Sanger

First presidential terms are all about open vistas—new programs to launch, new ideas, a new face to project around the globe.

Second terms are usually treacherous. Presidents find themselves living with the consequences of choices already made. And now, halfway into George W. Bush's second term, the central paradox of his presidency is that he has asserted greater presidential powers than at any time in history, took what he called a "thumping" in the midterm elections, and now finds his options more limited than ever.

The reason, in large part, is Iraq. Partisans and historians alike will argue for decades about whether the Bush administration invaded the country on false pretenses or was motivated by the noble cause of ending tyranny; whether the intelligence justifying the war was cherry picked; or whether military action was the best way to democratize the Mideast and end its days as an incubation ward for terrorists.

But there is little doubt that the scale of the mistakes made once the first "mission accomplished" phase of the war was over greatly has constrained Washington's choices. The rest of the Bush presidency will be consumed, one way or another, by the necessities of living within the political and economic costs of occupying, stabilizing, and getting out of Iraq. But only in the second term has it become evident how those costs go beyond money, blood, or the commitment of American resources.

While Bush and his stalwarts deny Iraq was a war of choice—in Tampa in February 2006 Bush told an audience that he believes Saddam Hussein "chose war"—several of those who departed the administration after the first term, from Colin Powell to Richard Haass, have said since that it was Washington that made the strategic choice.

But it was not until mid-2006 that the consequences of that choice became clear in the highest ranks of the Bush administration. The explosion of sectarian violence in Iraq and the failure of two plans to secure Baghdad made it clear that the administration would have to redefine its goals in Iraq—and would be lucky to get out without the country descending into a full-scale civil war. Iran's defiance of the United Nations and the nuclear test in North Korea have illustrated vividly how the commitment to Iraq has tied down Gulliver. At the White House and the State Department, no one can consider taking action beyond mild sanctions to end Iran's nuclear program without anticipating how the Iranians might retaliate across the border, perhaps through the Shia militias that they influence, perhaps by increasing the presence of Iranian agents in Iraq, some of whom are suspected of providing deadly technology for roadside bombs.

In North Korea the administration had poor choices before the missile and nuclear tests. But even after two UN Security Council resolutions calling for further isolation of the world's most isolated nation, the North Koreans paid little price. They appear to understand that Washington cannot risk another confrontation on the other side of the world. While the North returned to the negotiating table in December 2006, the country's strategy appears to be one of waiting out the end of the Bush administration. The Chinese have been increasingly helpful in managing the North Korean issue, but they also understand that an America consumed by problems in the Middle East is an America that cannot focus on the spread of Chinese political and economic influence in Asia—or advances in Chinese military technology such as the anti-satellite weapon the country successfully tested in January.

The Bush administration's push for democracy similarly has been undercut. The image of Iraqis voting for a permanent government was inspiring—as inspiring as the color revolutions that went before them. But the chaos that followed has not created the kind of example for the Middle East that Bush and Vice President Dick Cheney predicted. The Egyptians have calculated they can deflect the pressure for democratic experiments. The Saudis have masterfully used $60-a-barrel oil and an alliance with the Bush administration to deflect calls for liberalizations. Pakistan and Russia—two other nations Bush needs—brilliantly have turned their relationships with Washington to their advantage, knowing there is only so far Bush can push them. And because Iraq's daily dose of car bombings and sectarian killings play out on television screens around the world, it is hard for Washington to make the argument that political liberty is the shortcut to prosperity and stability. At this writing nearly four years after the invasion, Iraq's electricity service is not yet up to pre-war standards and its oil sector—which was supposed to pay for the rebuilding of the country—remains in shambles.

"It's not that we didn't have a plan," a top Bush aide told me at the end of 2005. "We had one. It was a good plan. It was not executed." That plan called for lopping off the top leadership of Iraq's military and its governing ministries and getting the country back to work by the summer of 2003. Instead, the military was disbanded, the ministries were left to wither, and American troops cleared neighborhoods and then moved on, only to watch the insurgents and militias move back in. They could never stay ahead of the violence. By the end of 2006, Stephen J. Hadley, the national security adviser, offered up a startling admission of failure:

> We could not clear and hold, Iraqi forces were not able to hold neighborhoods, and the effort to build did not show up. The sectarian violence continued to mount, so we did not make the progress on security we had hoped. We did not bring the moderate Sunnis off the fence, as we had hoped. The Shia lost patience, and began to see the militias as their protectors.

Moreover, Iraq has limited the president's options at home—dropping his approval ratings to the high 20s, levels not seen since Richard Nixon's presidency, and leaving few resources for new programs. Without question, the September 11 attacks would have propelled the budget on a trajectory of higher defense and homeland security expenditures. But the monetary cost of Iraq, the war of choice, has been stunning. By the end of 2006 it was a $450 billion effort, outstripping the Korean War (as measured in 2006 dollars) and beginning to approach the cost of the eleven-year struggle in Vietnam. Both those conflicts, of course, resulted in far greater American casualties. In early 2007 the Pentagon indicated that the cost of the Iraq war over the next year could exceed $8 billion a month.

So it was no surprise that Iraq triggered a political earthquake—the Republican loss of the House and the Senate. What was a surprise, however, is how quickly the American public turned against the Bush strategy of doubling his bet—and declaring that he was staying until victory is achieved. Congressional resolutions demanding withdrawal were seen as political suicide by the Democrats in late 2005. By early 2007, those calls were joined by some Republicans. And the next presidential election may well be fought on the question of whether to stay or withdraw.

Vision Interrupted

None of this was imaginable on January 12, 2001, when a fellow White House correspondent and I visited Bush on his ranch for a three-hour discussion of his vision for his presidency. That morning, while his two dogs barked just outside the living room of the old farmhouse on his ranch, then on a hike through the trails below, he talked of bringing a "Western mentality" to the White House and his hopes of a new era of bipartisanship. Saddam was a distant threat, only briefly discussed. The president-elect seemed to think he could deal with the dictator by remaking a sanctions regime that, he said that day, was so riddled with holes that "they resemble Swiss cheese." But he never discussed deposing him.

There was no mention of Osama bin Laden, no discussion of Afghanistan's role in harboring him or of any interest in bringing democracy to the country, by force or other means. When Bush turned to his plans for the American military, he talked at length about making sure that the American soldiers were never tied down in "nation-building" exercises, a frequent theme of his race the year before against Vice President Al Gore. It was impossible, he said, for American forces to be playing that role and at the same time deterring those who could threaten American security, or even pre-eminence. Asked whether America was more threatened by a strong China or a weak one, he stopped and queried his interviewer about whether this was a "trick question."

It would have been unimaginable to our host that day that six years later he would be engaging the American military in two huge nation-building efforts on a scale not seen since the rebuilding of Europe and Japan. Or that his call for a "humble" American foreign policy would have been overtaken so quickly with an American strike to topple the Taliban followed by the forcible ouster of Saddam and the president's own declaration, in his second inaugural address, that it was now America's mission to end tyranny around the world.

Today, that conversation just before Bush's first inauguration seems almost like a black-and-white newsreel from a different era, akin to talking to President Harry S. Truman in 1945 before the Russians set off a nuclear weapon or the North Koreans invaded the South. It is no accident that Condoleezza Rice, the secretary of state, has declared that this era is most akin to the Truman time, the days recorded in Dean Acheson's *Present at the Creation*, when America's relationships around the world were being reordered for half a century, when its global reach was being defined for the first time, and when it organized itself for a long struggle.

In the middle of Bush's second term it is far too early, of course, to assess what kind of long-term effects the momentous decisions that followed the September 11 attacks will have on America's standing in the world. That could take decades. Truman left office a seemingly semi-tragic figure, his poll ratings low, confidence in American leadership waning. It took decades for him to rebound in history's eyes. So perhaps it is no accident that the country's new respect for the feisty Democrat from Independence, Missouri, has become a favorite measure of comparison for White House officials seeking to shape the legacy of a feisty Republican from Crawford, Texas.

But it is not too early to begin to explore the ways in which the major decisions of the Bush presidency, and the major missed opportunities, have constrained Washington's abilities to reshape the world. There is no question that Bush's first six years in office have been a period of historic transformation. There is no question that he has disrupted the operations of al Qaeda and the proliferation ring run by Abdul Qadeer Khan, the Pakistani nuclear engineer. But there is reason to question whether, in the end, the strategy pursued thus far has positioned the United States to make the world safer.

Axis of Evil

Eight months after that interview at his ranch, Bush's world changed—and by his own account, so did his worldview. Before September 11, his presidency was about a range of domestic issues—lower taxes, smaller government, a new federal approach to education, and social conservatism—but it had no overarching central idea. It had an Eisenhower feel to it, this time with the president surrounded by a cast of neoconservative advisers who seemed to have a more activist agenda in mind than the president himself.

By the afternoon of September 11, all that had changed forever. Bush, still aboard Air Force One, and Cheney already had settled on the outlines of the declaratory policy that nations must choose between supporting the United States and supporting terrorists. (It was one of those clear precepts that fit the moment but could not stand the test of time—and did not.) Within weeks Bush had broad authority to pursue not only al Qaeda but its sympathizers and supporters. We now know that Bush and Cheney, who was particularly determined to expand presidential power, interpreted that authority to implement what was a plan to conduct wiretapping of any American suspected of being in contact with a member of al Qaeda, without the benefit of warrants.

Americans only learned of that order in late 2005, four years after the program began. But if the domestic spying was clandestine, the administration's fixation on Iraq was hardly a state secret. Historians may long debate whether the neoconservatives who held sway in the first term had set plans to depose Saddam before September 11 and simply used it as an excuse. Bush insists otherwise. During the investigation into the faulty intelligence about Iraq, he insisted that threats simply looked different after the attacks. Either way his direction was clear.

Four months after the attacks, in the 2002 State of the Union address, Bush famously labeled Iraq, Iran, and North Korea as an "axis of evil," words that many Americans read to suggest that the three had connected goals, if not a common strategy. By September 2002 there was a strategy in place to deal with the axis. Its public incarnation was the "National Security Strategy of the United States," written a year after September 11.

The strategy is best known for its assertion that the United States had a right—in fact, a defensive imperative—to strike first at any state or terror group that could harm the United States. Preemption is nothing new, of course; it goes back to the days of Daniel Webster, and it was the threat of preemptive military action that was the underlying steel behind President John F. Kennedy's approach to the Cuban missile crisis. But it always has been a tool, not a doctrine. Bush raised it to a new level.

He also built a deliberate ambiguity into the equation. When is a threat so severe that it merits a preemptive strike? And did Iraq meet that test?

Rice, still serving as national security adviser, conceded in 2002 that the administration was not using the classic definition of preemption—an act of self-defense when one sees an imminent attack in the making. She argued, persuasively, that in the post–September 11 age, such definitions are hopelessly outdated. In an era of hijacked airplanes and cyber war, armies no longer mass at the border. No threat seems imminent. Yet, at the same time, she did not want to advocate a policy of preventive war—striking an enemy when he is weak before he can become a major threat. Such wars have been condemned in history, and they have a dubious basis in international law.

So instead the administration crafted a new category, something between preemption and preventive war. For Bush, Iraq fit the new definition. The whole run-up to the war was all about making a case that a looming—if hard to pin down—threat to the United States made a classic case for preemptive military action. "Facing clear evidence of peril, we cannot wait for the final proof, the smoking gun that could come in the form of a mushroom cloud," Bush said in a speech October 7, 2002. And he did not wait.

We now know, of course, that the evidence was anything but clear and the peril was far from urgent. In fact, Saddam's military power began waning after the 1991 Gulf War, as Charles Duelfer concluded in his report about the search for illicit weapons. The same intelligence apparatus that had underestimated Saddam's progress in building a nuclear weapon before the Gulf War made the opposite mistake before the 2003 invasion. The result was that the first application of the preemptive war doctrine was missing the crucial element: an imminent threat, visible or not.

Wrong Order

The irony, of course, is that elsewhere along Bush's axis of evil, North Korea and Iran were racing ahead, building the weapons or gathering the technology that clearly fit the definition of a looming threat. The administration had been looking for its weapons of mass destruction in all the wrong places.

That reality raises a question the White House never has been willing to confront head on: Did the United States take on the axis of evil in the wrong order? Put another way, would Bush—and the United States—be in a different position today had North Korea been confronted first? Or Iran?

Rice rejects that theory. Saddam, she argues, had to be dealt with first because he was in a "bad neighborhood." The North Koreans, in contrast, are surrounded by democracies or allies or greater forces like China and have no recent history of lashing out. The Iranians, she said, before the election of President Mahmoud Ahmadinejad, were a society divided between hard-line clerics and a population drawn to the West and, ultimately, to democracy. To take military action there, she said, would drive the reformers into the arms of the mullahs.

Perhaps. But the result is that, six years into his presidency, Bush is confronted with nuclear threats that are far more serious than they were when he took office. In January 2003, as American forces were heading toward the gulf, North Korea evicted UN inspectors and withdrew from the Nuclear Non-Proliferation Treaty. The International Atomic Energy Agency immediately reported this action to the Security Council. The referral sits there to this day, untouched.

The North made no secret of its intentions. Within full view of American satellites, it began moving 8,000 spent nuclear fuel rods from a containment pond where inspectors had watched over them for nearly a decade. If reprocessed into plutonium bomb cores, that is enough fuel to build six or eight nuclear weapons.

Since then a succession of CIA directors has told Congress they believe North Korea turned that spent fuel into weapons fuel. While the size of the North's arsenal is a matter of debate, the North Korean nuclear test on October 9, 2006, ended any ambiguity about whether the country was a junior member of the nuclear club. Scientifically, the test was something of a fizzle, a sub-kiloton explosion that appears to have been far less than the four-kiloton test that the North Koreans told China they were planning to detonate. Politically, however, it demonstrated North Korea's "deterrent" capability.

The United States reacted by going to the Security Council and winning a resolution authorizing a series of new sanctions on North Korea, especially involving the search of its vessels and planes for illicit weapons. But South Korea, which had said that everything would change if the North proceeded with a test, has been enormously reluctant to embrace the sanctions, doing the least possible to comply with the resolution. Sanctions, it has determined, will only dig the North Koreans in deeper. China has been more helpful—it reportedly cut off oil to the North for a while after Pyongyang's missile tests in July—but it, too, fears pushing the regime over the brink. At the Asian summit in November 2006 in Hanoi, Bush pushed both Beijing and Seoul to entice or force the North to dismantle part of its nuclear infrastructure as a good-faith demonstration in advance of resuming talks. But at this writing, it is far from clear the North will comply.

It may be years before anyone knows for sure whether Kim Jong Il, the North Korean leader, sped ahead with his program and conducted the nuclear test because he believed Bush was distracted or because he believed Saddam's mistake was that he took on the United States before he had a weapon. He entered the six-party talks under pressure from China, but skillfully has dragged his feet, leaving the situation on the ground essentially as it was—except that he is continuing to produce nuclear fuel and thus, presumably, gradually is increasing the size of his arsenal.

But in the end Kim calculated that the United States could not risk a confrontation over North Korean nuclear ambitions while it is still tied up in Iraq. There were simply too many forces in the Mideast that would be needed if a crisis arose in the Korean Peninsula, meaning that as long as he did not precipitate such a crisis, the Bush administration would not. "The reality is that we had no good military options in Korea before Iraq," a senior administration official told me in late 2005, "and we have worse ones now."

In short, what Bush has lost on the Korean Peninsula is a credible threat of coercion. And that, in the end, is what the preemption doctrine is all about: the very real possibility that if diplomacy fails, the United States would seek to take out a nation's nuclear capability. Administration officials can argue, convincingly, that in a land of tunnel builders, that would never be a real threat in North Korea. But before January 2003 it was a significant threat. The United States knew exactly where those 8,000 rods were stored because of the UN inspectors who lived at Yongbyon for so many years. Early in 2003 the Pentagon, with no enthusiasm, presented Bush and Cheney with military options to keep the North Koreans from turning that spent fuel into weapons. They rejected the move as too risky.

Once the North was allowed to move them out of sight, either because Washington failed to lay down a red line or because it was distracted by Iraq, any credible threat of acting preemptively was gone. In North Korea, the preemption doctrine became an empty doctrine.

Iran is more complicated. Technologically the Iranians are years behind the North Koreans. Yet they have the resources—bolstered by high oil prices—to speed ahead with their own uranium enrichment facility. In 2006 they did exactly that, producing small amounts of uranium in defiance of a Security Council resolution demanding that they halt production. While sanctions were threatened, at this writing none have been imposed—largely because of objections from Russia.

Unlike North Korea, which boasts about its weapons capability, Iran claims its intentions are completely peaceful. But it never has been able to explain its covert dealings with Khan, who secretly sold centrifuge technology to Iran in the late 1980s and then again in the mid-1990s.

More important, the Iranians never have offered a convincing explanation of evidence found in a laptop computer, secretly provided to the United States by an Iranian, containing drawings of a warhead that appeared ready to receive a nuclear weapon. The weapon was missing from the thousands of pages of text and diagrams, but the text did describe a design for an air burst at the exact height for maximizing damage with a nuclear explosion. Repeated efforts by IAEA inspectors to obtain an explanation of those drawings, and the related "Greensalt Project" found in the computer, have been rejected by Iran for more than a year. In November 2006 the IAEA agreed to suspend cooperation with Iran on another element of its nuclear program, the building of a heavy water reactor, because it appeared to be too closely linked to weapons production. None of this proves that Iran has the bomb. But it does raise the question: why has Bush, who staged weekly events to remind Americans of the threat posed by Saddam, been so reticent about far clearer evidence involving Iran?

Again Iraq holds the key. The intelligence failures surrounding the search for weapons of mass destruction three years ago undermined American credibility when it comes to organizing the world to face a growing threat. Bush has acknowledged as much. The result is that the United States has had to distribute its intelligence information on Iran behind the scenes, hoping that the French, British, Russians, Chinese, and the Germans would conclude what Washington has. That effort has largely been a success—within the corridors of government. But it has been a failure in the public arena (except in Israel, which has mounted its own public campaign) because any intelligence gathered by the United States is now considered suspect.

The Iranians understand this and have exploited it brilliantly in Bush's second term. They have argued that they have a right to peaceful nuclear energy under the Nuclear Non-Proliferation Treaty, and unlike the North Koreans, they have been wise enough, at least at this writing, not to pull out of the treaty. So far there is no evidence they are building a weapon. In fact, most experts believe that what Iran seeks is a nuclear option rather than a bomb. It wants the capability that non-nuclear states like Japan possess: a stockpile of bomb-usable nuclear material and the engineering expertise to fabricate a weapon in short order, if the need arises. In short, it seeks a "virtual deterrent." Bush has said this is unacceptable, and he has responded to the two challenges, North Korea and Iran, by emphasizing that they can be solved diplomatically—as long as the diplomacy is accompanied by gradually rising pressure. In short, he is following the strategy that his harshest critics said they were looking for in Iraq—a gradual, multilateral effort to build up pressure. Bush has been careful to avoid any military threats to disarm either nation if diplomacy fails—even though, behind the scenes, the Pentagon is presumably constantly revising those options. The result has been that he has held together fractious alliances against both North Korea and Iran, in each case letting other countries take the lead. But the price has been high. Both countries have gained time to work on their nuclear programs with little impediment. In early 2007 the Bush administration clearly recognized that its Iran policy had been a failure. It began to confront the Iranians, conducting raids to seize Iranian operatives in Iraq, stationing two aircraft carrier groups off the Iranian coast, and cracking down on the bank lending Iran needs to develop its oil fields. While some fractures have emerged inside the Iranian leadership, the country has moved ahead, haltingly, with its nuclear program.

The question for the remainder of the Bush term is whether the president is simply biding his time, waiting for an international consensus to jell before taking more coercive action, or whether the quagmire in Iraq has made it politically impossible for him to act. The Iranians, like the North Koreans, seem to be betting on inaction, calculating that they are better off to race ahead with their nuclear projects now and deal with Bush's successor from a strengthened position.

Splits in the Administration

Iraq has had one other major effect: It has diminished the influence of the "neocons," the officials who urged American intervention to topple Saddam but miscalculated the cost of remaking Iraq.

The subtext of every struggle in Bush's first term was the battle between the differing factions of the administration. Secretary of State Colin Powell's State Department was conducting a daily rearguard action against Cheney and his staff and against Secretary of Defense Donald Rumsfeld and his office. The outlines of that struggle were known at the time; with the departure of key members of the administration, the details have been filled in.

In the second term Bush clearly decided to put an end to that internecine war. Powell left along with his deputy, Richard Armitage. But so did many of the ideologues. Rumsfeld's deputy, Paul Wolfowitz, took over the World Bank, removing from the cabinet debate a man who vigorously supported Saddam's ouster and was confident that oil revenues would pay for the reconstruction. Cheney lost his national security adviser, I. Lewis Libby, after he was indicted in connection with the investigation into the leaking of the name of a covert CIA agent, an event that grew out of the recriminations on Iraq. Others who played key roles in conceiving the Iraq strategy moved on. The day after the Republican defeat in the November 2006 elections, Rumsfeld was ousted and the president nominated as his successor a realist, Robert Gates, who was clearly brought in to alter the course Rumsfeld had set at the Pentagon.

The results in the first half of the second term have been evident. There has been little ideological butting of heads in Bush's second term—so little that some worry that the president is not hearing a true diversity of views. As secretary of state, Rice has been able to leverage her considerable influence with the president to implement some of the strategies, including an aggressive public diplomacy campaign that Powell could not get moving. Ideology is not dead. Bush has adopted the goal of spreading democracy as the rallying call of his presidency, and he waxes on about it in nearly every public speech and Republican fundraising event he attends around the country. But it is ideology without a military edge; while he talks of ending tyranny, he rarely mentions tyrants by name.

When efforts to destabilize a regime are conducted, they are usually thinly cloaked in other clothes. For example, American allies have little doubt that the effort to crack down on North Korea's counterfeiting of American currency and its shipments of drugs and missiles around the world are part of an effort to depose the North Korean regime. But no one in Washington dares say so for fear of triggering an open split with allies.

The same goes for Rice's request for $85 million to promote democracy in Iran. Until now the administration has been cautious about supporting dissident groups in Iran because any such effort could be interpreted as a plan to meddle in Iran's politics the way the CIA did before the 1979 Iranian revolution. No one in the administration uses the term "regime change"—the buzzword of the Iraq effort three years ago—to describe Bush's ultimate goal. Instead, Bush talks in folksy terms of building democracies. "Some day when you're old," he told a crowd in February 2006, he hopes Americans will look back and say "old George W. Bush and the United States Congress was right in keeping the faith that democracies can yield the peace we all want."

But that democracy building is also a hostage, at least in the short term, to events in Iraq. No Republican or Democrat wants to speak against building democracies. But the new split in the Republican Party is between those who believe they must endorse the strategy by endorsing Bush's strategy in Iraq and those who believe Iraq has become an albatross. Republican senator Chuck Hagel of Nebraska seemed to give voice to this when he said, in a profile in the *New York Times* magazine, "When I think of issues like Iraq, of how we went into it—no planning, no preparation, no sense of consequences, of where we were going, how we were going to get out, went in without enough men, no exit strategy, those kind of things—I speak out, I'll go against my party." He was not alone. A growing number of Republicans are now talking about exit strategies and abandoning the lofty early ambitions of a democratic Iraq that would beget other democratic states in the Middle East. Bush also changed his rhetoric, redefining victory down, even while rejecting several of the recommendations of the Iraq Study Group, including a declaration that, come spring 2008, American troops will be withdrawn.

Bush knows, of course, that Iraq will determine his legacy. He may be out of office for years before its outcome is known and the effects of his decision—and the mistakes made in the early days of the occupation—are fully understood. Historians will spend years debating why such a promising mission went so badly off course and to what degree it altered the trajectory of the rest of his presidency.

But one early conclusion seems clear even while Bush is still in office. His initial calculation—that a quick victory in Iraq would have a "demonstration effect" on dictators and nuclear aspirants around the world—seems to have been badly flawed. And the result is that, for now, other threats have flourished, leaving the United States to confront other nations that are building weapons and creating nuclear options that Saddam could only dream about.

5

Bush Foreign Policy: Grand Vision and Its Application

Carla Anne Robbins

Even for a president known for his idealism—or hubris to his critics—the ambition of George W. Bush's second inaugural address was breathtaking. In a twenty-one-minute speech that used the word freedom more than two dozen times, Bush declared that the spread of liberty and opposition to dictatorships was "the calling of our time," and he committed his presidency to the support of democratic movements and reformers "in every nation and culture, with the ultimate goal of ending tyranny in our world."

The breadth of that commitment stirred even the usually jaded Washington press corps. The *Washington Post* described a "profound break" from America's traditional foreign policy and alliances, while the *Wall Street Journal* declared it nothing less than an "end to *realpolitik*." At a minimum, to be true to his word, Bush would have to rethink America's relations with less than democratic allies such as Pakistan or Egypt. Some observers, mainly overseas, worried that Bush would go further, expanding his declared doctrine of military preemption to try to impose democracy forcibly on governments around the world.

The next day the White House walked it back.

In a hastily called briefing for a small group of reporters, one of Bush's top aides insisted the speech never was intended to signal a major change in U.S. policy or relationships. With an annotated copy of the address in his hand, the official emphasized other more cautious phrases: the president had said that ending tyranny would be the "concentrated work of generations" and "not primarily the task of arms." Strategically important countries such as Saudi Arabia, Egypt, Pakistan, Russia, and China already were taking some positive if preliminary steps toward reform, the official argued. "It is not a discontinuity, not a right turn" but rather "a bit of an acceleration, a raising of the priority" that the administration already had made of promoting freedom around the world.

The following day, a Saturday, Bush's father, former president George H. W. Bush, visited the White House press room and delivered a similar message, cautioning that "people want to read a lot into it—that this means new aggression or newly asserted military forces. . . . That's not what the speech is about. It's about freedom."

Bully Pulpit

The White House's surprise at the strong reaction to the president's speech says a lot about its insularity and how slow it has been to grasp the anxiety and mistrust generated by the Iraq war. The decision to walk it back—something that ever-disciplined aides insisted they were not doing—says even more about how the war has constrained Bush's options in his second term. Aides say the president is convinced that history will prove him right on Iraq, although progress may have to be measured in decades, not years. His commitment to the wider "freedom agenda" also is strong. But with more than 150,000 troops deployed in Iraq and billions spent each month to finance the war, he has very limited means to follow through. The Republicans' defeat in the 2006 midterm elections—which can be traced largely to public despondency over Iraq's spreading chaos—has further constrained Bush's ability to act, if not his certainty.

The presidential bully pulpit is a powerful thing even in a time of diminished means. A year after the speech, Bush's inaugural address was credited with changing the political rhetoric in the Middle East. Dennis Ross, an expert on the region and top aide to both President Bill Clinton and the first President Bush, said that this White House had put "democracy on the agenda. Even those (leaders) who hate the idea feel they need to look like they're embracing it." But Bush and his advisers were also reminded of how much a gamble democracy can be, particularly after the armed Islamist group Hamas—which refuses to recognize Israel's right to exist—won control of the Palestinian legislature. By early 2007, with Iraq spinning out of control, the president would embrace the region's autocrats—most notably Egypt and Saudi Arabia—in hopes of counterbalancing an increasingly powerful Iran. The president who had disdained the foreign policy realists for making cynical balance of power alliances found himself cutting the same sort of bargains.

Most of U.S. foreign policy in Bush's second term has been about learning to live within the limits of American power. After bullying its way through the first term, the administration—with Condoleezza Rice as the new secretary of state—has shown itself more willing to try diplomacy and its less-than-perfect compromises. After dismissing the United Nations and its subsidiaries as irrelevant and obstructionist, the United States teamed up with

France at the Security Council to isolate Syria. It allowed the International Criminal Court, a favorite first-term target, to take charge of investigating genocide in Sudan (although it has been unable to persuade Sudan to halt the killing or admit UN peacekeepers). The administration also dropped its campaign to oust International Atomic Energy Agency chief Mohamed ElBaradei (but not before ensuring he won a Nobel Peace Prize).

The shift has been most striking in Bush's dealings with North Korea and Iran. The president, who often leads with his gut, has made clear his personal distaste for both countries' despotic leaders, telling the *Washington Post*'s Bob Woodward that he "loathes" Kim Jong Il for his maltreatment of the Korean people. And if there were good military options, and the United States had the resources, either country might top the list for preemptive strikes or forcible regime change.

Instead, the administration cautiously has been backing multilateral negotiations—while also pressing for Security Council sanctions—to try to roll back both countries' nuclear programs. This is normal statecraft. But it is also a course Bush resisted throughout much of the first term, refusing to be associated with any deal that could be interpreted as legitimating or rewarding bad actors.

By early 2007 the administration's somewhat new course had produced mixed results. Iran was defiantly enriching uranium, months after the Security Council ordered it to stop. After the White House gave American diplomats permission to start a real negotiation with North Korea—including informal bilateral talks—Pyongyang agreed to move toward dismantling its nuclear weapons program. The deal was bitterly attacked by conservatives outside and inside the administration. But the president was clearly eager for some good foreign policy news and defended the agreement. It is impossible to predict whether it will hold.

Promised Humility

Governors who become presidents—including Clinton, Ronald Reagan, and Jimmy Carter—rarely have much foreign policy experience. But on the campaign trail with then Texas governor Bush, a perceived weakness in his knowledge of the world, fueled by some spectacular campaign flubs, became a metaphor for wider doubts about his intellectual gravitas. Bush sought to rebut those criticisms by highlighting his stellar cast of campaign advisers headed by Rice, a Stanford University Soviet expert. Characteristically, Bush never apologized for not being an expert himself, making clear that what he was offering was strong leadership while leaving the details to others.

Nothing from his presidential bid even hinted at an ambition to remake the post–cold war world.

While campaigning, Bush offered standard fare from the GOP's realist wing: He pledged to press ahead on missile defense, spend more building up the U.S. military, and be tougher on China and Russia. He was dismissive of nation building, and any talk of promoting democracy was laced carefully with caveats to make clear that U.S. economic and strategic relationships would come first. Iraq, or, for that matter, terrorism, was barely mentioned by either candidate.

When Bush talked about his style of leadership, he spoke of the need to temper America's vast power with "humility."

During his first eight months in office, Bush's agenda was even less ambitious, although his style had a lot more swagger than the promised humility. The foreign leader Bush seemed most interested in was Mexico's president, Vicente Fox. The top priority was getting out of the Anti-Ballistic Missile Treaty. And the organizing principle, says one official, was "if it looked good to the Clinton administration it needed to be rethought." Bush's new secretary of state, Colin Powell, got an early and embarrassing lesson about that—and a hint of his own personal troubles to come—when he made the mistake of saying publicly that negotiations on North Korea's missile program would pick up where the Clinton crowd had left off. The next day, Powell was sent out of an Oval Office meeting between Bush and his South Korean counterpart to tell reporters that North Korea was "a threat."

The administration also made clear its disdain for international treaties, defiantly rejecting the Kyoto treaty on global warming (the usually highly disciplined Rice shocked European diplomats at a luncheon by declaring the pact "dead on arrival"), the International Criminal Court treaty, the Comprehensive Test Ban Treaty, and a protocol to the biological weapons treaty.

It is also important to note that few of those agreements would have had much future in an Al Gore administration. But the Bush White House's unapologetic style provoked strong anxieties overseas, especially in Europe where the new president already was being caricatured as a dangerous cowboy. Bush's advisers were dismissive of the early criticism and even today seem surprised by its lasting effects. "Frankly we didn't consider any of [those treaties] 'alliance issues,'" said one official.

With Us or Against Us

Any U.S. president would have regarded the September 11 attacks as a mortal threat and almost certainly would have pursued al Qaeda and the Taliban with the same ferocity. It's less clear how many presidents would have sought to codify the lessons of 9/11 into a new declared doctrine of preemption or would have chosen to launch a second, even larger war in Iraq, especially without the United Nations or NATO along.

With September 11, Bush found his mission and his voice. "Freedom itself is under attack," Bush declared in a speech to Congress nine days after the attacks on New York and Washington. The war on terror "will not end until every terrorist group of global reach has been found, stopped, and defeated." And most memorably, "Every nation in every region now has a decision to make: either you are with us or you are with the terrorists."

The starkness of Bush's language and his unbending certainty reassured Americans at a hugely difficult time. It also forced many overseas leaders to make choices they were not eager to make. Pakistan's General Pervez Musharraf understood the threat and decided to side with Washington—and against his pro-Taliban intelligence services—providing support to the hunt for Osama bin Laden. Others further afield—Yemen, the Philippines, Georgia— also would join in, whether out of sympathy, fear, or a calculation of future benefit. Russian president Vladimir Putin agreed to have U.S. troops based in former Soviet republics and immediately grandfathered his own brutal fight against Chechen separatists into Bush's global war on terrorism.

Over time, the shock of September 11 would fade overseas. And that level of intensity and support would prove difficult to maintain without the sort of deft diplomacy the White House seemed too busy or too disinterested to engage in. There were early hints of troubles to come. On September 12—for the first time in its fifty-year history—NATO invoked Article 5, the common defense provision that is at the heart of the alliance. When Deputy Defense Secretary Paul Wolfowitz briefed NATO defense ministers in Brussels that same month about America's plans to fight the war on terrorism, he made no mention of a military role for NATO. In Washington, defense officials explained that many of the states around the table didn't have the equipment or the training to make a real contribution to the coming war in

Afghanistan, and their involvement only would complicate military planning. The Pentagon also had no interest in fighting a "war by committee" (a favorite and somewhat unfair criticism of the 1999 NATO campaign in Kosovo). European officials felt spurned by the performance.

Asked in a March 2003 interview about the reaction to his speech, Wolfowitz said that his position had been misread. At the time, the United States "didn't have any notion what kind of military forces we needed" for the forthcoming war to topple the Taliban "nor any notion that NATO as an alliance was prepared to commit to something as ambitious as Afghanistan." Still, Wolfowitz's deep mistrust of the Europeans was clear when he went on to note that he was rebuffed when he brought NATO a detailed proposal about how it could contribute to a likely war in Iraq. "But what we feared in September '01 is precisely what happened: the French blocked collective action," he said.

The speed with which the Taliban were brought down seemed to vindicate those early choices. In the months following the war, Bush would apply the same "with us or against us" standard to other issues—cutting off all relations with then Palestinian leader Yasser Arafat and dragging reluctant allies to the brink of a new war in Iraq, mainly by threatening to fight on his own.

While diplomats worried that the United States was alienating needed friends, White House officials argued that what they described as Bush's moral clarity—and disdain for diplomacy-as-usual—was what the world needed in such perilous times. "You have to let people know what isn't negotiable," Rice explained in a September 2002 interview.

Bush's impatience with diplomatic nuance became a running joke at the White House, one that aides eagerly recounted when asked about his operating style. "He'll say, 'Was that nuanced enough?' And then he'll turn to somebody and say, 'Nuance is a word that we use in foreign policy,'" according to an official who was a frequent target of Bush's digs.

And for a while the approach was remarkably successful. When Bush sought a preliminary UN resolution against Saddam Hussein in the fall of 2002, it passed 15-0—including yes votes from Russia, China, and Syria—in part because the United States agreed to return to the Security Council before launching a war but also because members were so relieved he had chosen to work through the United Nations rather than go it alone.

During those months there also were worrying signs of growing resentment toward the United States, even among long-standing allies. German chancellor Gerhard Schroeder salvaged his reelection bid by campaigning against a U.S.-led war in Iraq. Karsten Voigt, director for U.S. relations in the German Foreign Ministry, explained that his countrymen were not really against the idea of toppling Saddam. "For a lot of people I talked to, it was simply saying no to the U.S. that was popular."

White House officials rejected the criticism. Schroeder, they said, had betrayed the president—after promising Bush that he would not make Iraq an issue in his campaign. That Schroeder only months earlier had nearly lost a vote of confidence after pledging to send 3,900 peacekeepers to Afghanistan did not win him a pass with the president or his inner circle. "Doesn't he know I almost lost my government for him?" Schroeder later plaintively would ask his Washington ambassador.

Worrying Allies

In a June 2002 speech, as the Pentagon was readying for the invasion of Iraq, Bush declared a new strategic doctrine for the post-9/11 world. The strategy of deterrence that had held off the Soviet threat throughout the cold war no longer was enough to protect the country, he argued. Now the United States would have to pre-empt enemies. "If we wait for threats to fully materialize, we will have waited too long," he told cadets at the U.S. Military Academy.

Bush's declared intention to track down enemies inside sover-eign borders and even before they had marshaled their own forces for attack challenged the most fundamental premises of interna-tional relations. And it worried even sympathetic states that watched as the most powerful country in the world appeared to throw off the last constraints of international law. U.S. officials countered that America could be trusted to use its power and this new license wisely.

At the urging of British prime minister Tony Blair and then sec-retary of state Colin Powell—and despite the opposition of Vice President Dick Cheney—Bush decided to seek UN authorization before going to war against Iraq. (This time the Pentagon was eager for outside help.) But Bush also made clear that his patience with multilateralism was limited and that he was prepared to fight whether or not he got the United Nations' blessing. Bush cast the Security Council vote as a test for the United Nations' relevance rather than a judgment of his own decision to topple Saddam. "I believe when it's all said and done, free nations will not allow the United Nations to fade into history as an ineffective, irrelevant debating society," he declared in February 2003, a month before the start of the war.

The stark challenge that worked so well until then faltered in Iraq. For many states, the war against the Taliban was one of nec-essary retaliation. Iraq, by comparison, seemed to be a war of choice. The French and Russians (cheered on by the Germans, Mexicans, Chileans, and others) refused to go along.

Until the last moment, Bush's advisers predicted that Paris would blink (the French Defense Ministry expected that, too). When it did not, aides insisted that France and a host of others would be clamoring to join in once the war was quickly and felicitously won.

Within a few months of the war's end, White House officials tentatively began questioning at least some of those assumptions, according to a former aide to the president. By late spring 2003 it was becoming clear that there were no hidden weapons of mass destruction to find. American field commanders began to talk publicly about having to put down a second, more dangerous insurgent war—one that they clearly had not planned for. Officials particularly were shaken by the August bombing of the United Nations' Baghdad headquarters, which killed top envoy Sergio Vieira de Mello and left behind a smoking pile of metal and concrete frighteningly reminiscent of September 11. By the fall the White House began to acknowledge that it needed at least a limited UN blessing—both to legitimize the U.S. occupation and any new Iraqi government it managed to stand up.

Even then the administration could be disturbingly tone deaf. In December 2003, while Bush was lobbying for international help for everything from forgiving Iraq's official debt to training new security forces, the Pentagon issued contracting rules that barred all non-coalition members from bidding on billions of dollars' worth of prime contracts for reconstruction. Those who freely joined the Iraq war coalition also began to complain that the administration was far better at asking for favors than returning them. Eager to cement its standing as the most pro-American country in what Secretary of Defense Donald Rumsfeld had dubbed "new Europe," Poland sent 2,500 troops to Iraq. Still, when Warsaw petitioned the White House for a significant increase in military aid and a loosening of visa rules for its citizens to travel to the United States, the administration resisted. "You seem to be doing your best to estrange public opinion in friendly countries," warned then prime minister Marek Belka in a June

2004 interview. Belka had particular standing: until a few months earlier he was in Baghdad serving as finance chief for the U.S.-led Coalition Provisional Authority.

Historians will spend years trying to explain the gross mismanagement of post-invasion Iraq. Bush's national security team was one of the most experienced in recent memory, starting with Cheney, a former defense secretary, two-time Pentagon chief Rumsfeld, and Powell who had served as both a national security adviser and chairman of the Joint Chiefs. It is surprising that such a sophisticated crowd could be so easily deceived by Iraqi exiles—most notably Ahmed Chalabi—who persuaded them that invading American troops would be greeted as liberators and that Iraq had the political and economic infrastructure to quickly stand on its own. But that can only be part of the explanation. Rumsfeld's arrogant insistence on complete control and the White House's insularity certainly compounded the problems. Bush's lack of world experience coupled with an unbending certainty about his own moral rightness drove the entire effort forward—permitting very little internal debate and no real self-doubt.

In the 2004 presidential campaign, Democratic challenger John Kerry repeatedly accused Bush of causing lasting damage to the country's reputation and alliances worldwide. And he scored enough hits that a clearly uncomfortable president was forced to insist on his commitment to multilateralism and his close relationships with world leaders like "Vladimir" (Putin of Russia) and Belka's boss, Polish president Aleksander Kwasniewski.

The American public, polls showed, still trusted Bush more than Kerry to lead the war in Iraq and the war on terrorism.

Legacy Matters

The president and his advisers regularly compare these times, and their responsibilities, to the historic era that followed World War II.

With a clear eye on his legacy, Bush told supporters in a second-term speech that he was "absolutely convinced that some day, fifty or sixty years from now, an American president will be speaking to an audience saying, 'Thank goodness a generation of Americans rose to the challenge and helped people be liberated from tyranny.'" Rice noted in an opinion article that she had hung a portrait of Truman's second secretary of state, Dean Acheson, in her office, writing that "like Acheson and his contemporaries we live in an extraordinary time—one in which the terrain of international politics is shifting beneath our feet and the pace of historical change outstrips even the most vivid imagination."

But there is no mention these days of Bush's doctrine of preemption, for which the Iraq war has turned out to be a particularly poor test case. Richard Haass, president of the Council on Foreign Relations and a top State Department aide in the first term, says any shift likely had more to do with a change in "context than any change of hearts or minds. . . . The great irony of this administration is having fought a war of choice" in Iraq, it now finds it has very limited choices for action.

When asked how to understand the changes in the second term, current officials offer differing explanations. Some say it is part of a natural progression as the United States moved from fighting two wars to what they hoped would be the demands of postwar rebuilding. A few acknowledged that the United States had alienated too many friends, and those relationships had to be repaired. One aide said the biggest change was that, this time, "Condi wins."

To understand the evolution of Rice's thinking, that aide also recommended that I look at the writings of Yale historian John Lewis Gaddis. (Gaddis was one of several experts brought in to speak with White House officials as they were readying Bush's second inaugural address. Gaddis was also awarded the National Humanities Medal.)

In a January 2005 article in *Foreign Affairs* magazine, "Grand Strategy in the Second Term," Gaddis praised Bush for presiding over what he calls "the most sweeping redesign of U.S. grand strategy since the presidency of Franklin D. Roosevelt." And he endorses military preemption as an essential and lasting change in U.S. doctrine. "Neither Bush nor his successors, whatever their party, can ignore what the events of September 11, 2001, made clear: that deterrence against states affords insufficient protection."

But Gaddis also is highly critical of the administration's failure to "legitimize their strategy" of preemption and to win wide international consent for the war in Iraq. "From nearly universal sympathy in the weeks after September 11, Americans within a year and half found their country widely regarded as an international pariah," Gaddis wrote. Having shattered an outmoded international system, he argued, Bush must now patiently build a new one—one that will make clear to the world that it is better off with the United States in charge. Gaddis then counsels the administration to develop "better manners," to refrain from insulting potential allies, not to "regard consultation as the endorsement of a course already set," and to work to gain "multilateral support for the preemptive use of U.S. military power."

With Rice as secretary of state, the administration has developed better manners. As the United States tried to woo Pyongyang back to the table, Bush even referred to North Korean leader Kim Jong Il as Mr. Kim. But any change has been grudging at best—a concession to America's limited options rather than an embrace of compromise.

New Thinking

When Bush chose Rice to be secretary of state, the conventional wisdom was that the hard-liners had won. With Powell gone there would be no one with the stature or the wiles to counterbalance Cheney and Rumsfeld. Rice, while personally close to Bush, rarely challenged either of those men in the first term. Her own convictions were opaque, even for many on her staff, as she played the role of honest and very private broker to the president. Rice's aides say that is the role Bush wanted her to play, much as Brent Scowcroft had for the first President Bush. They also acknowledge a key difference from those days: The first Bush also had a very powerful secretary of state, James Baker, with whom he was extremely close. For reasons of ideology, personality, or perhaps implicit rivalry, Powell always was seen as an outsider.

The balance of power in the second term has turned out differently as Rice assumed a role (if not a worldview) very similar to Baker's.

Even before the midterm elections—and his ouster from the Pentagon—Rumsfeld's star had been tarnished, with White House officials privately blaming him for overselling the ease of the war and badly managing its aftermath. In the second term, he dedicated most of his energy to "military transformation." Cheney remains one of the president's closest advisers and his most opaque. But his office took a serious blow when his powerful chief of staff, I. Lewis "Scooter" Libby, was indicted for allegedly lying to prosecutors about his role in the leaking of the name of a CIA operative who also was the wife of a vocal Iraq war critic. Rice's successor as national security adviser, her former deputy, Stephen Hadley, gladly plays an even quieter and more private role.

While Powell disliked foreign travel (and for good reason, since whenever he left Washington either the White House or Pentagon managed to publicly undercut him), Rice appears to revel in it. Her staff keeps close track of how many miles she's logged—and how many more than Powell. Still, some foreign officials caution that the change from the first term may not be as great as it appears.

"They take a lot more meetings, but they still tend to lecture more than they listen," said a European diplomat.

Rice has assembled a policy team whose political instincts have far more in common with the first President Bush's administration than the current Bush's first term. How much the State Department ("the building" as it is called) is influencing Rice is hard to tell. But she is a natural achiever—from playing near concert–quality piano, to competitive ice-skating, to becoming provost of Stanford University before she turned 40. Being the country's top diplomat has likely made her and the administration more diplomatic.

The choice of Europe for Bush's first post-inaugural visit was a clear effort to soothe relations. Still, when Rice preceded the president by a few weeks, she sounded as brusque as ever—sharply dismissing European suggestions that the United States throw its support behind negotiations with Iran. On the flight over, she told reporters that Tehran's human rights record "is something to be loathed." She continued that tone in both public and private, calling the Iranian regime "totalitarian" and saying the United States would do nothing to legitimize the mullahs.

A few weeks later, after Bush's tour of the continent, Rice's team would modify that position. In return for a European pledge to bring Tehran to the Security Council should negotiations fail to restrain its nuclear program, Washington agreed to drop long-standing U.S. opposition to Iran's bid to start accession talks with the World Trade Organization. Still, when French, British, and German officials suggested to Bush and Rice that the United States might push the process forward further with a hint of interest in improving bilateral relations, they were firmly rebuffed.

Asked to explain the shift in Rice's thinking, one official says that the secretary was surprised and disturbed when on nearly every stop of her visit she was asked whether the United States was planning a military strike on Iran's nuclear complex. "We kept hearing it everywhere we went: from officials, from the foreign policy elite, from students. It's not what we expected," the aide recalls. Again administration officials seemed remarkably unaware of the effect they had on others. Just a few weeks earlier, Cheney had suggested that the United States might not be able to stop Israel from attacking Iran's nuclear facilities.

Rice, who often was criticized in the first term for lacking strategic vision, also has championed the administration's most ambitious new diplomatic overture: bringing India finally and completely in from the cold by agreeing to sell it civilian nuclear technology.

The administration had strong strategic and mercantilist reasons. India is the biggest democracy, has a good nonproliferation record—except, of course, for its own illicit weapons program—and could be an important counterweight to China if handled correctly. The White House also is eager to revive the U.S. nuclear industry with new overseas markets until the American public is brought around. But the deal also has broken the fundamental rules of the nonproliferation regime at a time when the United States is depending on those rules to help rein in North Korea and Iran.

Promoting Democracy

After elections in Iraq, Afghanistan, and Lebanon, Bush and his advisers were eager to claim credit for what they said was a rising tide of democracy in the Middle East.

The administration quickly received some sharp reminders of how difficult promoting democracy can be, particularly in a region where—even with a fair vote—the good guys don't necessarily win. The Palestinian legislative election was the most shocking to the administration even though both the Israelis and the moderate Palestinian leadership privately had suggested to the White House that the vote should be postponed to head off a near certain Hamas win. Bush still said no. Bush and Rice further undercut America's influence when they did nothing to restrain Israel's ill-fated air war against Hezbollah in Lebanon. Hezbollah was bloodied but not broken while the Lebanese people (and most Arab moderates in the region) blamed the United States for the suffering and widespread destruction. Even then, it took the threat of a resurgent Iran and a desire to curry favor with the region's conservative Sunni Arab governments to persuade Rice to volunteer her good offices to try to revive peace negotiations between the Israelis and Palestinians. Rice continued to insist that there was no "linkage" to the Iraq war, but her aides made clear that the administration was desperate to rally as many friends as possible.

Congress's sudden rebellion in late 2005 over Iraq—coupled with a sharp drop in Bush's approval ratings—caught the White House completely off guard. Public support for the war had been steadily draining away as elections failed to stem the violence and the number of U.S. deaths and casualties mounted. The White House made things far worse with a series of missteps over the summer and fall, most notably the disastrous mishandling of Hurricane Katrina. In the days after 9/11 Bush had captured many Americans' imagination and trust with his firm commitment to track down and destroy America's enemies. Now many began to question whether Bush was capable of protecting the country, at home or abroad. When Representative Jack Murtha (D-Pa.), a decorated Marine and respected voice on military issues, called for a withdrawal of U.S. troops from Iraq, the White House lashed back wildly. Press Secretary Scott McClellan declared that Murtha was embracing "the policy positions of [*Fahrenheit 911* filmmaker] Michael Moore and the extreme liberal wing of the Democratic Party." Bush later would call Murtha "a fine man, a good man."

But for a White House that takes pride in its iron grip on "the message," things were beginning to spin out of control.

By the fall of 2006, the chaos in Iraq would drive Bush's approval rating down to the 30s and Republicans out of the leadership of both the House and the Senate.

Bush, who continues to insist that victory is still possible in Iraq, appeared more shaken by the election results than by all of the previous months of horrifying front-page stories out of Iraq. Pentagon planners were ordered to review military strategy. Rumsfeld was ousted from his job and a "realist" from the first President Bush's administration, former CIA chief Robert Gates, was brought in to replace him.

Hopes in Washington and around the country for finding a sensible way out of Iraq were pinned increasingly on the recommendations of the bipartisan Iraq Study Group headed by Baker and former representative Lee Hamilton (D-Ind.). Another realist alumnus from Bush 41, Baker is a legendary dealmaker and as temperamentally different from Bush as can be imagined. The unanimous report provided Bush with the political cover to begin winding down America's costly presence in Iraq. The central point of its 79 recommendations was that the White House should focus far more aggressively on training Iraqi troops and prepare for the withdrawal of American troops, with all combat brigades to be out by early 2008. The report also set out a clear set of political milestones the Iraqi government needed to meet if there was to be any hope of tamping down the civil war and said Washington should reduce its military and economic support if Iraq's leaders continued to resist. And the report called on the White House to begin an aggressive round of regional diplomacy—including talks with Iran and Syria—in hopes of enlisting their help in containing the war.

In early January 2007, Bush went on national television to outline his new strategy for Iraq. While he said that he had "benefited from the thoughtful recommendations of the Iraq Study Group" he took very few of them. The president announced that he would be sending another 20,000 troops to stabilize Baghdad, and he warned Iran and Syria against further meddling in Iraq. And while he warned Iraqi leaders that America's "commitment is not open-ended" he refused to impose any timetables for their embrace of political reforms or for the withdrawal of American troops.

Bush appeared strained and his rhetoric was much toned down from his second inaugural address. But the fundamental themes were still there. He declared that what America is confronting across the Middle East was "the decisive ideological struggle of our time." He declared that "in the long run the most realistic way" to protect Americans is "to provide a hopeful alternative to the hateful ideology of the enemy." And that, he said, could be done, "by advancing liberty across a troubled region."

6

Governing Executively: Bush's Paradoxical Style

Charles O. Jones

The presidency of George W. Bush is fascinatingly paradoxical. It features many firsts, mosts, and leasts, thus making it difficult to compare or analogize to other presidencies. Prominent among these distinctions is this paradox: the president with the least political standing of those elected in modern history is among the most boldly aggressive policy advocates. Seemingly where narrow-margin politics appears to call for sensitive mastery of Congress, Bush employs an unrelenting executive style, among the most intense ever. He governs executively, often ignoring what are judged by observers to be his limitations. Additionally, he has been beset with unanticipated crises that require executive responses, a need to fix accountability, and that raise doubts about competence.

These observations are apparent from Bush's time in the White House, though his six years as governor of Texas also provide evidence of his preference for an executive governing style. Having won a less disputed second term, it was unlikely he would alter his approach; quite the reverse.

It is frequently said that there have been several Bush presidencies. That may be true in terms of agenda-bending events like 9/11, the war in Iraq, corporate scandals, a dramatic rise in oil prices, and devastating hurricanes. But Bush's style of governing has changed little from the time of his inauguration on January 20, 2001. Adjustments made along the way are typically within an executive manner, not toward another style.

In elaborating these contentions, this chapter discusses the firsts, mosts, and leasts of the Bush 43 presidency; clarifies the president's weak political standing; differentiates executive and legislative styles of governing; provides historical examples of these styles; specifies the Bush executive style and how he defines it; illustrates the mix of competition and cooperation in lawmaking during the first and carrying over to the second term; notes the effect of crises for an executive style; and provides concluding observations regarding the effects of a pure executive style.

Firsts and Rarities

Analysis of the special features of the Bush presidency starts the day after the 2000 election. The firsts and the rarities are familiar:

—The election did not settle who won in the first such case since 1876, when an electoral commission was convened by Congress to resolve disputed returns from Louisiana, South Carolina, and Florida.

—The U.S. Supreme Court effectively determined the winner for the first time.

—The Senate was tied, a first since 1880.

—First all-Republican government (president and Congress) since 1952; second since 1928.

—An unusual election map: Democrat in the Northeast and on the West Coast, with a midwestern peninsula dropping down from Canada; Republican in the rest of the country (a map virtually duplicated in 2004).

The terrorist attacks on September 11, 2001, were even more important in shaping the Bush presidency. They had dramatic effects on the agenda, decisionmaking, the public psyche, and the presidency. A primarily domestic agenda, managed by a primarily domestic-oriented president, instantly was transformed into one in which national and homeland security issues were paramount. Military action in Afghanistan and homeland security measures elicited bipartisanship; other domestic proposals unrelated to 9/11 did not.

The magnitude of change in public approval of the president was historic. His quarterly average in the Gallup Poll was 55 percent before 9/11; it was 87 percent in the final quarter of 2001. Bush also maintained higher ratings for a longer period than any president for whom we have such numbers. The public's approval of Congress also improved dramatically during this time.

There were other firsts and rarities in Bush's first term:

—A switch in party control of the Senate during a congressional session (May 2001).

—Passage of legislation usually associated with the Democratic agenda: education reform, campaign finance reform, a prescription drug benefit.

—A preemptive war in Iraq—an action based on faulty intelligence and division among NATO allies.

—First full-term president in the modern era not to use the veto.

—First president since Franklin D. Roosevelt in 1934 and 1936 to have his party experience net gains of seats in both the House and Senate in a first midterm election and in his subsequent reelection.

—Reelection by the smallest popular and Electoral College margins since Woodrow Wilson in 1916.

—Least turnover in the modern era among cabinet secretaries in a first term followed by the highest turnover at the start of the second term.

—Presentation of the boldest and highest profile second-term agenda of any president since FDR in 1936.

—Narrow-margin politics at the beginning, as evidenced by close party splits in Congress and razor thin wins by the president.

Least Political Standing

Narrow-margin politics relates to an altered political climate in which presidents work. Split-party governments were common from 1969 to 2003. Of the seven presidents serving during this time, only Jimmy Carter (four years) and Bill Clinton (two years) had one-party governments. With growing Republican strength in Congress from 1992 to 2006, narrow margins also were featured. The average party split in the House for this period was 219 Republicans, 214 Democrats; in the Senate, it was 52 Republicans, 48 Democrats. The mean popular vote percentage for Clinton and Bush (1992 to 2004) was just over 48 percent. Of the four elections, only the one in 2004 produced a majority for the president. Not surprisingly, congressional party unity increased as leaders, including the two presidents, had to work hard at winning support from their members.

How can presidents rally support? On entering office they can point to two types of hard numbers: their electoral margins (popular and Electoral College percentages) and the initial reading of job performance, presumably reflecting the public's forecast of their success. Adding these three percentages produces a composite number that permits a ranking and comparison of political standing upon entering office among the post–World War II presidents.

Of the fifteen elected and reelected post–World War II presidents, Bush ranked dead last when he was inaugurated in 2001. He displaced himself when he was inaugurated in 2005. In other words, he established a new "dead last." His percentages of the popular and electoral votes increased slightly, but his job approval declined.[1]

Bush fares little better in comparison with all reelected presidents in history, in this case combining only the percentages of the popular vote and Electoral College vote. There are thirteen reelected presidents from the time of recorded popular vote in 1824 to the present. Of these thirteen, Bush ranks twelfth (Wilson was just slightly lower).

The other reelected presidents in the postwar period (Dwight D. Eisenhower, Richard M. Nixon, Ronald W. Reagan, and Clinton) easily won second terms. But none of these four more comfortably reelected and positively evaluated presidents at reelection had as active and bold a second-term agenda as Bush. Perhaps his self-assurance was related to a second set of hard numbers: the status of his party in the House and Senate. By these measures, he ranked seventh and fifth in legislative standing of the elected and reelected postwar presidents. Of the four other reelected presidents, only Eisenhower and Clinton ranked higher in legislative standing upon election but ranked lower in this category at their reelection.

Bush's executive style aided him in overcoming weakness in political standing and in capitalizing on legislative standing. There is a paradox to explain: that is, how relatively high system productivity can result during a presidency that has limited public support and questioned professional reputation. Perhaps narrow margins and intense competition, possibly even loathing, motivate lawmakers to act. There are political risks for an executive-style president in responding to crises. Whereas a crisis necessitates executive action, seemingly a plus for the Bush orientation, it concentrates accountability in the presidency. There is no escape.

Different Styles

Executive and legislative styles of governing are distinctive. They may be discussed as pure styles, understanding that practically they are best understood as a continuum.[2]

A pure legislative style is representative, reactive, responsive, collaborative, open and sharing, compromising, and narrowly accountable to constituencies. Representation is the key to understanding this style. Legislators, or presidents using a legislative style, view issues from the perspectives of their constituents, reacting and responding accordingly. If a law is to be enacted, legislators must develop means for collaborating and compromising. But bargaining diffuses accountability. Who made this law? Answer: Lots of us. Therefore, behaviorally, legislators are accustomed to sharing accountability and culpability with others. The effect of their standard working life is to avoid command, and thus liability.

A pure executive style is proactive, hierarchical, contained, programmatic, resolute, and broadly accountable. Enterprise is the key to understanding this style. Hierarchy is established both symbolically and practically to promote initiative and accountability. It also provides the structural containers for defining problems, planning, and making choices. That is not to suggest that interests are not represented in the executive world, only that the process of getting information is orderly, routinized, and often less transparent than in the legislative world.

Executives tend to be more programmatic than legislators, making an effort to relate one proposal or policy to the next. That tendency, along with hierarchy, also fosters more resoluteness than flexibility in supporting a plan or decision. In marked contrast to the legislative style, executive behavior invites command and its attendant risks and liabilities.

Another aspect of representation is critical in distinguishing the more legislative from the more executive method. As with legislators, a representative-conscious executive like Clinton seeks personal support from the public, essentially as confirmation of status. An enterprise-oriented executive like Bush seeks policy support from the public. For the first, representation is integral to the development of proposals. For the second, proposals are developed within the executive hierarchy, which are then to be promoted by the "team" on Capitol Hill and to the public.[3]

Executive Background of Presidents

One naturally looks first at the background of presidents in distinguishing between executive and legislative styles. The record for the forty-three presidents shows twenty-one with all or mostly executive backgrounds, eighteen with all or mostly legislative backgrounds, and four with a balance. Further, twenty-nine presidents were in executive positions when elected or taking over (as vice presidents), three were in legislative positions, and eleven were in private life. Of the twenty-nine in executive positions, nineteen were elected and ten were appointed (mostly in the cabinet or military).

Which presidents, by background, offer the best comparisons with Bush? Surprisingly, there are very few. Here are the criteria from Bush's background to look for: elected (not taking over as a vice president), reelected, all executive experience in previous posts, and in a civilian executive job at the time of his election as president. Two presidents in addition to Bush meet these criteria: Wilson and Clinton. Reagan comes close, but he was in private life when he was elected. Each of these four presidents had experience as governors, Wilson the least, Clinton the most.

Additional cases for comparative purposes can be drawn from those with mostly executive backgrounds: Thomas Jefferson, James Monroe, and Franklin Roosevelt. Of the takeover presidents, only Theodore Roosevelt had a mostly executive background. These four presidents also served as governors. By historical criteria, Bush is among the purest executives to serve as president. But there is contemporary evidence for this contention associated with Bush's own concept of the job. And that evidence provides space between him and Clinton, less between him and Wilson.

Bush's Pure Executive Style

In his analysis of presidential power, Richard E. Neustadt identified three principal sources of presidential power as persuasion: "His vantage points in government, together with his reputation in the Washington community and his prestige outside."[4] Elsewhere I specify the first source as position, defined as the "vantage points in government" combined with the qualities and expectations of the presidency as shaped by the public, the media, others in government, and the president. Together these attributes of position contribute to the status of being president.[5]

Bush scored low on two of these three resources. His reputation in the Washington community was questionable at best. Many doubted his competence and qualifications to serve as president. These critics also questioned his legitimacy for being there in the first place. Being mostly impressionistic, reputation is not easily enhanced. It is also subject to partisan filtering, especially so in narrow-margin politics. Doubts about Bush's competence and legitimacy have persisted throughout his time in office, even during the period of high job approval following 9/11.

Bush's public prestige suffered initially from his having lost the popular vote and having just barely won Florida to give him a four-vote victory in the Electoral College. Still, his initial job approval rating at 57 percent was seven points more than his popular vote and was exactly the average of initial job approval ratings of Reagan, Bush 41, and Clinton when they first were elected. It seems that the public is more positive than negative about a new president regardless of his electoral margin.

In summary, upon entering office Bush's principal sources of power were position and a job approval rating that offered encouragement more than prestige. However shaky his reputation and prestige, Bush, not Al Gore, took the oath of office on January 20, 2001. He would therefore move into the White House, make executive appointments, designate the agenda, determine its sequence, sign bills into law, issue executive orders, and serve as head of state and commander in chief.

Position is the key source for the executive-oriented president. It provides occupancy at the very pinnacle of the executive hierarchy. Authority and organizational, even governmental, dependency come with that tenure at the top.[6] The president has the right repeatedly to say yes, no, or try again. And so other power holders come to the White House whether or not the president has impressive public prestige and professional reputation.

For their part, executive-oriented presidents are likely to boost a strength rather than bolster a weakness. For Bush, that meant building a team of loyalists—"Team Bush," as one scholar expressed it.[7] For if reputation and prestige are unlikely to improve, then organizational support may contribute to exceeding expectations. And expectations for presidents with lesser reputations and limited prestige are likely to be low. Oddly, weaknesses under these circumstances can be advantageous by lowering the bar for an executive team and thus allowing it to exceed expectations if conditions and capabilities permit.

Bush behaved from the start in accordance with his conception of the presidential position. Even as the Florida recount was proceeding, Bush was forming his presidency, not knowing whether he had won. Confident that he would prevail, he asserted his responsibility to organize. Dick Cheney was designated shortly after the election to manage the transition. Once the Supreme Court made its decision favoring Bush in *Bush* v. *Gore,* the cabinet and major White House staff were named in short order—just seventeen days. Likewise, an agenda was specified, with priorities designated and plans for an issue-a-week promotion announced. These actions were tagged as "arrogant," but they provided early evidence of Bush's executive style of governing.

By these actions, Bush sent clear signals even before Day One regarding his conception of presidential leadership. Whereas analysts expected, and some recommended, caution, even humility in exercising power, Bush appeared to define the job in terms of goals to be achieved and responsibilities to be exercised, mostly ignoring advice from outside the team to consult Democrats for purposes of coalition building.

The pure executive defines the job more proactively by tasks than by constraints. The principal questions for the executive are: What has to be done? What did we say we would do to get the job? Of lesser importance is the question: What limits our doing it?

This style is less attentive to the more collaborative dimensions of policy and lawmaking. It also tends to be less forbearing of the more purely legislative style in providing lessons for how to make decisions. In its most generous interpretation, the executive attitude is you do your job, I'll do mine, and let's try not to do each other's. A less generous version is either go along or stay out of it.

The task emphasis of the executive style does not ordinarily begin with coalition building. Bush is fond of saying that he won't negotiate with himself. In regard to Social Security reform, he observed that he is not a member of Congress. These statements aid in defining his interpretation of position as power, which is as a pure executive. It is his responsibility to designate issues and make proposals that he judges to be the correct ones, not to compromise in advance of the workings of Congress. By this view, changing a proposal to suit criticism before it is introduced makes no sense. To do so imagines that the president knows what will happen in Congress, not to mention conceding in advance a change that might later attract support in the form of real votes.

Virtually by definition, a president favoring a purely executive style is unlikely ever to adopt a legislative style. But this ultra-separationist perspective does not exclude accepting a compromise later. Rather, it questions the effectiveness of proposing a deal in advance of a counterproposal or signals from Capitol Hill as a bill works its way through the legislative process.

Cooperation and Competition

Should a president with weak political standing, one forced to rely primarily on position, work cooperatively with the other party? Several analysts recommended that course of action during and after the disputed 2000 election and again following the narrow win in 2004. Yet bipartisanship was unlikely to happen for many reasons, almost all associated with a six-year period of bitter partisan conflict during the Clinton presidency and carrying over to the 2000 and 2002 elections. Consider these developments, then ask if cooperation was likely in 2001 or 2005:

—The Republican takeover of Congress in 1995 and the partisanship that ensued—the so-called Gingrich revolution.

—The partial closing down of the government in 1995 as congressional Republicans battled Clinton over the budget.

—The impeachment and trial of Clinton contributing further to partisan bitterness.

—The disputed result of the 2000 presidential election, including the unprecedented intervention of the Supreme Court.

—The net increases for Democrats in the House and Senate in 2000.

—Republican control of Congress by narrow margins in each house, a condition likely to encourage discipline in both parties.

—A shift in party control of the Senate following Vermont senator Jim Jeffords's switch to independent status in 2001.

—A controversial resolution authorizing the use of armed force against Iraq in 2002.

—An extraordinary net increase in House and Senate seats for the president's party in 2002.

—A bitter and personal presidential campaign in 2004.

—A narrow win for the president in 2004, with charges of voting irregularities, accompanied by net increases in House and Senate seats for the president's party.

These circumstances favored competition, not cooperation. The 2000 results, along with those in 2002 and 2004, are the latest manifestations of narrow-margin politics that have been a feature of national governing since 1993. The switch of a small number of votes in presidential elections and a few congressional seats can change which party is in charge of which institution. Conclusion: the stakes are high when the margins are close and neither party is likely to start by conceding very much to the other. The contrast with large-margin politics is striking. During Lyndon B. Johnson's presidency, minority party incentives were few. Why try? Narrow-margin politics stimulates party incentives on both sides of the aisle, sometimes resulting in a bitter partisanship unsettling to those desirous of harmony.

What has been the record of competition and cooperation in lawmaking during the Bush presidency? It is a pattern so special that it will occupy scholars for some time to come. Here is a much-too-abbreviated overview:

—First five months: competition with presidential advantage (tax reform passes).

—Next three months: competition with Senate Democratic advantage (Patients' Bill of Rights passes Senate).

—Post-9/11: cooperation with presidential advantage, serving as commander in chief (flood of legislation—use-of-force resolution, emergency spending, homeland security, education).

—2002: cooperation on security measures, competition on pre-9/11 agenda (energy, faith-based initiative, tort reform)

—2003 to 2005: competition on full agenda—national security and domestic issues.

Analyzing these patterns will necessarily include the differences between the House and Senate. The rules in each chamber call for different strategies. House rules give the majority significant advantages if party discipline holds, and it did during the first term. Thus, whereas the minority House Democrats had incentives to participate actively, the majority Republicans often shut them off. Straight partisanship trumped competitive partisanship in that chamber throughout Bush's first term.

In the Senate, any minority with over forty members has significantly more checking, delaying, and obstructing powers than even a 49 percent House minority, again as long as majority party discipline is maintained there. The so-called "hold" and the threat of a filibuster give the Senate minority leverage in bargaining on legislation. Therefore, the president often has had to work at getting Democratic votes.

The usual lawmaking sequence has been for legislation to move from the tightly controlled House to the Senate. Bush has been notably successful in getting partisan support in the House, with a proposal passed there going to the Senate, often with a partisan tone. Changes made in the Senate to accommodate the minority Democrats often were unlikely to be favored by House Republicans, thus sometimes resulting in contentious conferences or stalemate.

Competition is an expected and healthy enterprise in presidential-congressional relations, especially in a period of narrow-margin politics. The partisan bitterness that is displayed need not prevent the passage of major legislation. In fact, the record shows substantial legislation having been enacted: tax cuts, education reform, campaign finance reform, prescription drug benefits, bankruptcy reform, the Patriot Act, corporate accountability, fast-track trade authority, election reform, creation of a Department of Homeland Security, and a comprehensive energy package. Seventeen major legislative acts were passed in the first two years of the Bush presidency—the second highest among first-term presidents in the post–World War II period.[8] Sometimes it is useful to look beyond the daily coverage of conflict to the end product.

Bush's Concept of Leadership

The Bush concept of leadership stresses an executive style that has remained consistent through his service as governor and president. There are several sources for this: Bush's book, *A Charge to Keep* (prepared for the 2000 presidential campaign and written mostly by Karen Hughes); an interview with Bob Woodward for his book *Bush at War;* an analysis by Hugh Heclo regarding Bush's "political ethos"; and a press conference following his reelection in 2004. I begin with the last.

It was the president's view in 2004 that the voters extended the chief executive's contract for four years, and that act served as an endorsement of his policy intentions.

"When you win, there is a feeling that the people have spoken and embraced your point of view, and that's what I intend to tell the Congress, that I made it clear what I intend to do as president . . . and the people made it clear what they wanted, now let's work together," Bush said.[9]

In his mind, his election victory provided affirmation, not only for him but also for Congress. He saw his campaign as asking "Should I do these things?" The voters said yes. That response, for him, is the essence of political capital. Again quoting Bush:

"I earned capital in the campaign, political capital, and now I intend to spend it. It is my style. I'm going to spend it for what I told the people I'd spend it on, which is—you've heard the agenda: Social Security and tax reform, moving this economy forward, education, fighting and winning the war on terror."[10]

What about cooperating with the Democrats? The president provided a classic executive response: "With the campaign over, Americans are expecting a bipartisan effort and results. I'll reach out to everyone who shares our goals."[11]

That is about as tightly argued as a rationale can be: I won. You lost. That's behind us. Let's get down to work on the winning program—mine.

Bush's impressions of the purposes and effects of campaigns were not invented for the 2004 presidential election. This is what he wrote in 1999 about winning reelection as governor of Texas; it has a familiar ring:

"Politics is not about the past or rewarding officeholders for a job well done. Voters want to know a candidate's view for the future. I had earned political capital by doing in office what I said I would do during my first campaign. Now was the time to spend that capital on a bold agenda for change and reform in the second term."[12]

This lesson, among others, was learned by Bush-the-son as a participant observer in Bush-the-father's campaigns. It was apparent that the son believed that the father did not capitalize on his successes in the Gulf war for promoting his domestic program.

There is another striking similarity in Bush's second-term viewpoint between Austin and Washington. He wrote in 1999: "I didn't come to Austin just to put my name in a place card holder at the table of Texas governors. I came to do what I thought was right."[13] This theme was repeated in 2004: "I really didn't come here to hold the office just to say, 'Gosh, it was fun to serve.' I came here to get some things done, and we are doing it."[14] Bush clearly views himself as a purposeful executive.

Bush also wrote about the differences between executive and legislative styles in his book, expressing the distinctions cited earlier. The leaders of the Texas legislature were characterized as "horse traders."

"The legislative process is one of give-and-take, of agreement and disagreement. Their job is to figure out how to shape and mold legislation, to put together the pieces into a whole that can gather enough votes to pass.

"My job is different. A Governor is a chief executive officer. I believe my job is to set its agenda, to articulate the vision, and to lead. . . . The Governor has the power of the bully pulpit, the ability to communicate with the public to articulate a message, an idea, an agenda. A Governor sets a tone. . . . A strong person can make a powerful difference."[15]

Many other facets of Bush's concept of executive leadership are revealed in Woodward's interviews with the president, as cited in *Bush at War*.[16] Some samples:

—"I think my job is to stay ahead of the moment. . . . be the strategic thinker that you're supposed to be."

—"One of my jobs is to be provocative. . . . to provoke people."

—"I like clarity [in lines of responsibility]."

—"A president has to be the calcium in the backbone. If I weaken, the whole team weakens."[17]

Many of these declarations also are expressed in Bush's book, especially those regarding relations with staff. He likes order, discipline, access, loyalty, no leaks, confidentiality—all in support of a "team" organizational concept.[18]

Heclo traces the Bush executive style to a political ethos reaching back to family and personal growth.[19] Family fostered a sense of duty and a testing of character bolstered by support of those who had been there before—notably his grandfather, former senator Prescott S. Bush of Connecticut, and father, former president George H. W. Bush. Performance motivated by duty and responsibility suggests nobility, which, in turn, protects one from criticism, or, at a minimum, from the need to answer critics. Yet it also may induce isolation from and limited tolerance for the less nobly inspired lawmakers—that is, constituency-oriented members of Congress.

Next for Heclo was the emergence in the late twentieth century of a kind of high-tech, permanent campaign, take-no-prisoners politics. As the next generation Bush, George W. was schooled "in this new world of polls, consultants, media relations, and the selling of political personas" by Lee Atwater, father Bush's political consultant.[20] At the very least, this apprenticeship prepared Bush to appreciate the talents of Karl Rove.

Heclo questions how one could navigate the cultural and mood changes of the latter decades of the twentieth century. His response? "In a culture increasingly heavy with the complexities of self-examination and doubt, Bush refused to get lost in nuances. He honed his natural instinct to cut to the heart of the matter . . . while generally staying on whatever ground was well known to him."[21]

Finally and most importantly, Bush found that discipline enhanced willfulness that, in turn, fortified and sustained obligation (thus fulfilling the family ethos). It was here, Heclo argues, that religion played a role. It helped to discipline his willfulness and to seal himself off from transient politics—that which dominates Washington. Perhaps this personal security in family and religion explains why Bush is disliked by the intelligentsia. How can they possibly like someone who prefers Crawford, Texas, to Washington, D.C.? Though less hated, and probably less threatening, Carter and Reagan were in this same tradition.

Preemption, Hurricanes, Accountability

Governing executively invites accountability. President Harry S. Truman declared, "The buck stops here," thus encapsulating the very essence of hierarchy. Bush's view of lawmaking is separationist: he proposes, Congress disposes. He acknowledges the need for compromise but is much less forbearing of cross-institutional or inter-party consultation. Measured by the passage of major legislation, the record during his tenure is impressive, if nearly always highly contentious.

But there is another record, that of crisis response, in which separationism is less apparent or even less likely to occur. Crisis favors executive decisionmaking, relying as it does on hierarchy and extant authority. Responsibility is, therefore, concentrated. Elected executives are expected to lead and to be accountable for their decisions and those of their subordinates. Typically, executive performance is tested by polls significantly more often than is legislative performance, with presidents evaluated the most frequently.

Bush's term in office has witnessed several crises, the most notable being 9/11, the war and insurgency in Iraq, soaring oil and gas prices, natural disasters, and the threat of nuclear weapons development in Iran and North Korea. In the case of 9/11 and two monster hurricanes (Katrina and Rita), the president reacted, cooperating with local and state officials. Preparedness was vital to the response. The threat in each case was apparent (terrorism and hurricane warnings), but the exact sites and magnitudes were uncertain, as was the method in the case of 9/11. The administration's response to 9/11 received high marks, the responses to the hurricanes low marks. The judgment regarding nuclear power in Iran and North Korea is pending. The increases in gas prices were incremental before Katrina, when the Gulf Coast refineries were shut down. But prices spiked again in 2006 with insecurities in several oil-producing countries.

The war in Iraq is a crisis of a different order. Bush associated the need for military action to the broader war on terrorism and thus was reactive in that sense. Strictly, however, the action was preemptive, not reactive—a move taken to prevent terrorism or its support from a regime said to have weapons of mass destruction. This was a case of assuming responsibility in advance of aggression, not meeting public expectations for executive leadership in a crisis. The public was unaware of the threat said to exist by the president. Therefore, the public (and Congress) had to be convinced of preemption, as most were in the early phases of the war.

Both reaction and preemption involve substantial risks for the executive-style president. Certain crises, as with 9/11 and unprecedented hurricanes, are of a magnitude and rarity that preparations are bound to be inadequate or inapt. Yet the president, by position (reinforced by style in Bush's case), is a magnet for accountability regarding the effectiveness of reactions. Preemption carries even more risks for the executive. As an action-forcing move, it places a premium on being right, both in the rationale for and the effectiveness of the encounter. Errors made release those, like members of Congress, from responsibility for their having been misled.

Conclusion

The Bush presidency is special for how it came into being, what it has tried to accomplish, and the agenda-bending events that have occurred, as well as the outsider status of a president serving on the inside and the pure executive style exhibited by the president. Even at this early stage, certain features are apparent in helping to explain his seemingly paradoxical style:

—As a president entering office with low political standing, Bush has capitalized on position—the status of being president—in proposing a bold agenda. Reputation and prestige have been less important in how he defines the job, though seemingly vital to perpetuating low expectations of his performance.

—The president's concept of his responsibilities is borne of his political background and personal experience with family, friends, and cohorts. His perspective is less dependent on the Washington community than its members would prefer.

—Bush is a pure executive as president, among the truest in history of those with civilian backgrounds and among the most policy-active of those with either civilian or military backgrounds.

—Purity of form typically provokes and maintains separation from other styles while fostering competitive lawmaking in an era of narrow-margin politics.

—Fidelity to a pure form induces conformity by members of Congress to classical representation, thus requiring the executive to campaign outside for influence inside. Bush regularly has campaigned for his policy priorities, with mixed success.

—The Bush presidency has been beset with crises that oblige executive leadership and fix accountability in the White House. However suited to the pure executive, such crises carry risks of eroding presidential power, including position, the resource relied on most by Bush.

The prospects for a successful presidency during the final two years of Bush's term depend on changes in fortune in regard to issues for which the president will be held accountable but over which he has limited control. These issues have had a negative impact on his job approval ratings and likely will limit his influence on the domestic priorities he identified at the start of his second term. Democratic victories in the 2006 congressional elections further dimmed prospects for the president's agenda. Although Bush will not be a candidate in near-term elections, the issues preoccupying his presidency will be featured in those contests and beyond.

Notes

1. Charles O. Jones, *The Presidency in a Separated System,* 2d ed. (Brookings, 2005), table 2-3, p. 52.

2. Charles O. Jones, "Bush v. Kerry: Questions about Governing Styles," Policy Brief 134 (Brookings, June 2004).

3. George C. Edwards III, *Governing by Campaigning: The Politics of the Bush Presidency* (New York: Pearson Longman, 2006), ch. 8.

4. Richard E. Neustadt, *Presidential Power and the Modern Presidents* (New York: Free Press, 1990), p. 150.

5. Charles O. Jones, "Capitalizing on Position in a Perfect Tie," in *The George W. Bush Presidency: First Appraisals,* edited by Fred I. Greenstein (Johns Hopkins University Press, 2003), pp. 174–75.

6. For perspectives on what has been labeled "unilateral powers," see the special issue of the *Presidential Studies Quarterly,* vol. 35, no. 3 (September 2005), devoted to that subject.

7. Donald F. Kettl, *Team Bush: Leadership Lessons from the Bush White House* (New York: McGraw-Hill, 2003).

8. David R. Mayhew, *Divided We Govern: Party Control, Lawmaking, and Investigations, 1946–2002,* 2nd ed. (Yale University Press, 2005), pp. 212–13.

9. Dan Balz, "Ready to Govern in His Own Style," *Washington Post,* November 5, 2004, p. A5.

10. Mike Allen, "Confident Bush Vows to Move Aggressively," *Washington Post,* November 5, 2004, p. A1.

11. Balz, p. A5.

12. George W. Bush, *A Charge to Keep* (New York: William Morrow and Company, 1999), p. 218.

13. Ibid., p. 123.

14. Allen, p. A1.

15. Bush, *A Charge to Keep,* pp. 118–19.

16. Bob Woodward, *Bush at War* (New York: Simon & Schuster, 2002).

17. Ibid., pp. 136, 144, 244, and 259.

18. Kettl, *Team Bush.*

19. Hugh Heclo, "The Political Ethos of George W. Bush," in *The George W. Bush Presidency: First Appraisals,* edited by Fred I. Greenstein (Johns Hopkins University Press, 2003), pp. 17–50.

20. Ibid., p. 45.

21. Ibid., p. 45.

Contributors

Dan Balz
Washington Post

John C. Fortier
American Enterprise Institute

Fred I. Greenstein
Princeton University

Charles O. Jones
University of Wisconsin
(emeritus)

Norman J. Ornstein
American Enterprise Institute

Carla Anne Robbins
New York Times (formerly
with *Wall Street Journal*)

David E. Sanger
New York Times

Index